ABSOLUTE

MOTIVATION

Battle-tested Principles

for Next-Level Living

**JAMES
DIXON**

Absolute Motivation

Battle-tested Principles for Next-Level Living

James Dixon

Copyright © 2023

ISBN: 979-8-9859524-6-9

All rights reserved. No part of this book may be copied, reprinted, or reproduced in any way, electronic or otherwise, without written permission from the author and/or publisher.

Joint Venture Publishing

Blue Sky R&D, LLC

Events and experiences described in this book are based on the author's recollections and are not intended to represent word-for-word transcripts. Rather, the author has retold them according to his memory. In all instances, the essence of the dialogue and/or situation is an accurate representation of the author's recollections.

No warranties or guarantees are expressed or implied by the inclusion of the content herein. Neither the publisher nor the author shall be liable for any physical, psychological, emotional, financial, or commercial damages, including, but not limited to, special, incidental, consequential, or other damages. The reader is responsible for their own actions and results.

Printed in the United States of America

CONTENTS

Foreword 5
Superman is Born 7
Slurs at Three 9
Rocks 11
Emmett 13
Introduction to Shriners 15
Matt and Gilbert 19
The Amputation 23
The Trophy 27
Hulk Hogan 31
Back to Indiana 35
Phys Ed Class 37
Jordans 39
My Father 45
Siblings 49
Basketball 55
Heaven's Gates and Hell's Flames 57
A New Me 63
Another Run at Basketball 69
AAU 75
Benedict Arnold 77

Senior Year	83
College	85
Almost Left College	91
Brian	95
Razor's Edge	99
Transferring to Bob Jones	101
Post-College Plan	111
Marriage	119
Daughter Arrives	121
Brooklyn Tab	123
Grandma	127
Finding My Way Back to Faith	131
Revival	135
The Fall	141
"Secular" Work	145
The Race	151
Workplace Ministry	153
The Prosthetic Company	155
Advice for the New Amputee	163
Superman	169
About James Dixon	176

FOREWORD

Every day, we see people with impressive stories, but few have had as many obstacles as James Dixon. Born with a physical disability, James's childhood was marked with racism, ridicule, disappointment, and repeated defeat. Yet James never gave up. With undying faith, he steadfastly persevered and claimed victory over adversity.

Simply put, if anyone has epitomized the concept of turning challenges into opportunities, it is James Dixon.

This book is his testimony. His experiences are sometimes humorous, while others are tragic. From childhood to the present day, however, he has strived to be a victor, rather than a victim. If you ask James how he does it, he will credit his faith for helping him find his purpose.

From sports to spirituality, James shares his life experiences in this book. As an amputee, he has denied his disability and conquered it, while turning to the ministry, where he also experienced rewards and setbacks. Through it all, his admirable mindset shines through and serves as a source of inspiration for the people who know him.

Yes, James lost his leg, but in that loss, he found his purpose. He is a superhero to other amputees, and he is a voice for the disabled and disadvantaged. He is proof that the seemingly impossible is possible and that faith is our most faithful companion.

You are about to meet a real-life Superman. His name is James Dixon, and this is his incredible journey. Let his story serve as your inspiration to find your own superpowers and use his battle-tested principles to take your life to the next level.

Dr. Greg S. Reid
#1 Bestselling Author, Speaker,
and Founder of Secret Knock

SUPERMAN IS BORN

"For you created my inmost being; you knit me together in my mother's womb. I praise you because I am fearfully and wonderfully made; your works are wonderful, I know that full well. My frame was not hidden from you when I was made in the secret place, when I was woven together in the depths of the earth. Your eyes saw my unformed body; all the days ordained for me were written in your book before one of them came to be."
(Psalm 139:13-16)

God had been fearfully and wonderfully designing a baby boy for nine months, and in August of 1973, James Eltroy Dixon was introduced to the world at St. John's Hospital in Anderson, Indiana. He was complete with bright eyes, an adorable smile, ten little fingers, and ten little toes. His mother was overjoyed with her adorable little arrival.

Then it was noticed that his right thigh didn't look quite perfect.

The doctors determined he had a slight fracture and splinted his leg. There was no reason to suspect that there would be an issue with it healing, so he was free to go home with his mom.

As time passed, the leg didn't heal, so at the age of three months, he had his first surgery. Unfortunately, surgeries became a regular thing as the quest continued to figure out how to help James be mobile and engage in activities like any other child. While the repeated surgeries caused scar tissue to build up in his leg, scar tissue was building up in his heart as he struggled to be accepted by other children.

Mom and Grandma were determined to instill in James a belief in himself. As part of their mission, they bought him Superman clothing and toys. Even though he was physically limited and disabled, they were determined that there would be no limits on him. They were building in him the belief that he could do anything.

He was being groomed to be Superman.

SLURS AT THREE

Hospitals were becoming a regular part of my life. When I was three years old, I spent time at a children's hospital in Indianapolis for yet another round of surgeries. My mother and grandma could not be there with me the entire time, so I was left in the care of the nurses. One nurse had been referring to me with a particular term, one that was new to me, so I thought nothing of it.

One day, my mother and grandma came to visit, and as they walked in, I said, "Here comes my nigger momma."

My mother and grandma were shocked. The term "nigger" was never used around my home or among my neighbors.

My grandma had a quick reply, "Whoever told you that, their momma is a nigger." No one responded to her comment.

There I was at the age of three being exposed to my first racial slur, but I lived in Indiana, and that was the culture at the time.

Communities were still very segregated; yet I was not being brought up that way. Skin color never mattered to my grandma—her door was open to anyone. Like my grandmother, skin color didn't make a difference to me. I grew up playing with other children without any consideration of skin color.

I can only imagine the lack of confidence in the medical professionals that began growing in my mother and grandma. These were supposed to be educated professionals. How could they use that derogatory term, especially around a child? Given the racial slur, they had to wonder if these medical professionals were really looking out for my best interests. Were they really trying to do their best to help me, or was I just someone to practice on?

ROCKS

I wanted so badly to be like the other children. Sometimes, though, that led to less-than-ideal choices and some memories that make me laugh today.

The children in the neighborhood had started throwing rocks at cars. It was not really done with malicious intent but rather just to pass the time. I so wanted to join them in doing it, but I couldn't run and was barely able to walk. Even though I'd undergone surgeries and rehab, I was very limited. One day, though, I decided to join in the "fun."

With the help of a little walker, I made my way out to the curb in front of my grandma's house. I was determined to throw rocks just like the other children; however, I wasn't able to run away to avoid being caught, like they did. I also couldn't get a good aim when I was standing at the curb, so I had to move closer to the cars. I had to literally go out into the street and be right next to a car in order to hit it.

Imagine you are the guy who sees this child with a walker, a crippled kid, coming out into the street and hitting your car with a rock. Then you watch as the kid tries to escape, but he can't run. He can hardly walk. Of course, he is moving ever so slowly, directly in front of the house where he lives. Obviously, he wasn't going very far.

The gentleman got out of his car and literally followed me, walking just as slowly as I was, as I tried to escape. I couldn't climb the steps very well, so he actually helped me up the steps so I could "get away from him." Even though the guy I was escaping from was helping me, I was proud of myself, thinking I was really getting away. I can only imagine how humorous it must have been to watch the scene play out.

Of course, he told my grandma what I had done, and while I'm sure he wasn't happy that I'd thrown a rock at his car, he amazingly said, "You know, I am not even mad, not even at the little crippled kid who was throwing rocks at my car. He was out in the road, and I was afraid I would hit him."

The man had mercy on me that day.

EMMETT

When I was in the third grade, Mom worked at the Boys' Club. I was often picked on, so she would take me along to the Boys' Club, hoping it would be a better environment for me. When I was there, I watched other children my age go upstairs to do karate and wrestling. With the brace on my leg, it was challenging for me to ascend the stairs, but I figured once I'd made it up the stairs, I could fight another child who was about my size.

I had sized up Emmett and was convinced I could take him. I remember my mom saying, "James, do not mess with Emmett. He is older than he looks. Just because he is little, that does not mean you can beat him."

Being a typical boy of about eight or nine, I didn't listen to Mom and went upstairs to the wrestling mat.

I attacked Emmett, and that was it. That kid was strong. He surprised me by picking me up in the air and bringing me down to the mat. Having been so sure I could take him, I didn't understand how he'd been able to bring me down so fast. His arms were so short it didn't seem possible to me. How did he get so strong? I didn't know, but I knew I wanted him bad. No longer believing I could take Emmett, I chose another route—I wanted him thrown out.

The next thing Mom knew, I was coming back down the stairs.

"Mom, Mom, kick Emmett out. Kick Emmett out!"

Emmett had just shown me that I should not underestimate him just because he was little. In my defense, this was the first time I'd met someone with dwarfism. Until that day, I didn't know that a person with a diminutive stature could be an adult. In my ignorance, I believed I surely could beat that kid, only to find out he was not a kid at all.

And my mom has tried to warn me, but because I wanted to be like the other kids and do the things they did, I chose not to listen.

INTRODUCTION TO SHRINERS

Until I was eleven years old, I continued to have surgeries almost every six months. One of my thigh bones was growing faster than normal to compensate for the shorter leg. They had tried taking a bone from my rib cage and putting it with my femur, but that was unsuccessful. The bottom half of my right leg was just not growing properly, and growth spurts only served to aggravate the challenges.

Nothing the doctors tried was working, so I wore buildups that added inches upon inches to the bottom of my right shoe. I had locking braces, but that was like being an above-the-knee amputee with an immobile knee, so in order to walk, I had to swing my entire leg forward. That severely limited my ability to run and keep up with the other children.

The children's hospital I visited regularly had run out of possible solutions and never did get it right. Looking back, I feel as if they were experimenting on me, trying different things, hoping something would work. The 32 surgeries I have had in my life that had kept me from walking, running, and being like every other child were, in the end, 100% unnecessary.

It just so happened (or we might call it God's providential hand at work) that I had a neighbor, an older white gentleman who happened to be a Shriner, who lived across the street from my grandma. After noticing how often I sat and watched the other children play, he came over and initiated a conversation with my grandma. He told her the Shriners help little crippled boys. My grandma put him in touch with my mom, and he told my mom that the Shriners would love to take me in to see if they could help me. He said they would even take care of all my medical bills for free. It sounded too good to be true, but at this point, there was nothing to lose. If there was even a small chance that they could help me, it was worth trying.

When we got to the Shriners Hospital in Chicago, my mom and dad went into an office, while the staff put me in a wheelchair and took me on a tour. They showed me the whole place, and it was so fun and awesome that I felt like I was in Disneyland. At the end of the tour, I remember thinking how cool it was.

Up until then, my life's medical experiences had started with what they thought was a broken leg that did not heal, followed by more than a decade of surgeries that never led to an actual solution. Now, the Shriners were giving my mom hope, all because the neighbor said he wanted to help a crippled boy for free. No one had ever told me what was wrong with me, but the Shriners were finally able to truly diagnose the problem as poor circulation. Bones require a good supply of oxygen and nutrient-rich blood in order to grow.

The bones in my right leg were not getting enough of that life-giving blood.

Many more visits to Shriners would follow as they determined the best plan forward for me. For the first time, there was hope that something could be done to help me.

I remember feeling left out whenever I'd watch all the kids playing in the grass. During one of my visits to Shriners, I told Grandma, "I want to do something." While she didn't know what I wanted to do, she hoped my request was not too big because she cautioned me, "You know you have a big surgery coming up."

"I want to know what grass feels like," I said.

It was such a simple request, but I don't think anyone had ever realized that I'd missed out on something most people take for granted. Hearing my request, they didn't hesitate to carry me out and let me put my feet in the grass. It was the most amazing feeling! I had never felt the grass beneath my feet like that before. For me, it was a big "WOW" moment to feel the sensation of that perfectly manicured grass underfoot.

I had been enjoying one of those visits to Shriners and was sitting in a room in a wheelchair when both my mom and dad walked in. I can remember this moment well because I was not used to seeing them together. Their relationship had dissolved years earlier, and it was only because they needed to sign documents for my medical procedures that they would both be present together.

That day, my dad wore a necklace around his neck. It had the letter "E" on it, which was the first initial of his name, which was Elmer. He took it off and put it around my neck and said, "If you ever need me, put this in the mail, and I will come to you." I didn't know what was happening when he said that, but it was the first thing I can ever remember him giving to me that meant something.

Then, my mom stood in front of me in the wheelchair. My nickname was "daddy" because they said I was an old soul, wise and all that other adult-like stuff. She said, "Daddy, I need you to be good. I am going to be back. As soon as I can, I am going to be back. I will be here with you."

It was at that moment that I found out that they were leaving me. I was going to be alone in this hospital, which was four hours from home.

I was accustomed to Mom leaving and going to work, but it never bothered me because Grandma was always there. This was the first time that Grandma wasn't going to be there. Outside of Mom, the biggest connection in my life was Grandma. She was significant to me. She was not there, and they were leaving me. On some level, I didn't think much of it. Time was not something that registered to me at that age, and I didn't know what I was there for or for how long. However, I was accustomed to going in for surgeries, so I thought I would see them the next day. But that wouldn't be the case this time. Given the extensive surgeries that had been attempted to date and the vast amount of scar tissue, the Shriners' recommendation was to amputate. I was not yet aware of that. I was only thinking I was going in for another surgery, something I was used to. Little did I know that this surgery wouldn't be anything like the rest—it would be life changing.

MATT AND GILBERT

I was taken to the Great Lakes wing of Shriners Hospital in Chicago. There, I learned I would have two roommates, a child named Matt and a child named Gilbert.

Matt was in an incubator to the right of me. He was eight years old, white, and had two parents. His mom and dad were great. They were there all the time. Matt had a bone disease and was severely deformed and undersized. Everyone was always trying to give him milk, and his family would reach into the incubator with gloved hands to interact with him. I remember that he had a lot of toys, particularly stuffed animals. He was fragile, but he had a great personality.

Gilbert was to the left of me. He was 12 years old—older than I was. Gilbert was paralyzed from the neck down, the result of a fall in the Cabrini-Green projects in Chicago. He had a halo that kept his head stationary, so he did not have a lot of movement and was always on his back. There were a lot of limits for Gilbert.

The three of us became friends, and we enjoyed talking, particularly at night. he hospital staff put a mirror on the ceiling so we could see each other's faces when we talked. Since I was in the middle, I would sometimes have to relay what Matt was saying to Gilbert and vice versa. It was fun.

With Matt being in an incubator, he wasn't mobile. He couldn't walk over to me, but when I would leave the room to go to rehab, I'd stop at his incubator and talk to him.

Then one day, Matt was not in the room. His mom and dad came over to me and gave me one of his stuffed animals and said, "Thank you for being his friend." I remember Matt's parents being so loving toward us and so thankful. I didn't quite understand that he had died or what that really meant. I didn't understand that kids die. It was my first time facing death at all.

Then, it was just me and Gilbert. A few days after Matt died, Gilbert's mom came in to visit. She closed the curtain between us for the first time to give them privacy, but our mirror was still on the ceiling. She said, "Gil, I need you to listen to Momma." He said, "I'm listening, Momma. I'm so glad you are here. This is my friend, James…"

"No…Gil." She sped past everything he was saying because she had something to say to him. "Gil, Momma can't do this no more."

I remember him asking, "Do what, Momma?"

She said, "I just can't do this. This is eating up my life. I can't keep coming out here. Listen, I can't do it no more. These people are gonna take good care of you, but I can't do it."

She kissed his head, and then she left the room for good.

Gilbert became upset and cried out to her, "Momma, I won't be bad no more." Then he yelled, "Mercy Momma, Momma, have mercy, Momma..." He kept begging and pleading, "Please, please..." Then, totally distraught, he tried to hold his breath, take his life, bite his tongue, and do anything he could to just stop breathing. That's when it hit me—kids die, and your family leaves you.

I asked the nurse for an envelope, and I put the necklace my dad gave me in the envelope.

"What do you want me to do with it?" she asked.

I told her that my dad said if I put that necklace in the mail, he would come get me. When the nurse told me that he hadn't left an address and thus it would never get to him, my sense of hope began to die.

I still didn't know what they were going to be doing to me, because no one had yet told me.

THE AMPUTATION

One morning, I remember them giving me a bath, and they told me to use a special soap on my bad leg. I still didn't know anything about the planned surgery. No one had mentioned it to me yet. At one point, though, my mom had asked me previously if I wanted to lose my leg. I replied, "No," so I thought it was my choice. After that, no one brought it up again. I never heard another word.

Then they took it. When I woke up, my leg was gone.

I asked if I could see the portion of my leg they took from me before they took it away, and they actually let me see it. As I looked at it lying in front of me on a cold metal table, I remember trying to see if I could move it or reconnect with it. It was strange to see my leg there in front of me, but somehow separate from me. It was like attending a funeral alone.

I certainly hadn't expected this to happen, so I was understandably in shock and disbelief at my loss. I was too young to know how to grieve, and no one was with me. I had no loved ones or family members to comfort me or help me understand what I was feeling. I was just eleven years old and did not understand how to process everything that was going on inside.

None of my family members had made it there yet. All alone, I was very hurt and angry. When the doctor came in, I tried to swing my pillow at him out of anger. I felt like he took something from me, and, in fact, he had. But no one had prepared me for it.

The nurse tried to reassure me. She kept telling me I could do anything. I could accomplish anything. I could play basketball one day. She was trying to encourage me, but I was really terrified that no one was coming, and, like Gilbert, I'd be all alone. I had lived through the trauma of Matt's dying and Gilbert's mother leaving him, and I was beginning to understand the trauma of loss. In my mind, there were only two possibilities: I was either going to die, or my family was all gone Forever.

However, when my mom got off work, she drove the four hours from Anderson, Indiana to Chicago. When she heard about my behavior and outbursts, she came into my room quite upset. There were certain rules and expectations that were always placed on me, no matter what. There was a level of respect that I was to have at all times because I was the child and these were adults. My behavior toward the doctor was disrespectful, and this was unacceptable to my mom because doctors were to be held in high regard. She felt I needed strong correction. While she had overheard the nurse telling me about all the things I could learn to do, she wasn't yet in a place to believe that and felt I needed a dose of reality.

She said, "Son, you are a cripple. You are going to have to learn to use your mind."

For me, this was all unacceptable. This was different than simply being disrespectful to adults or doctors, for that matter. I was not being disrespectful for the sake of being disrespectful. I felt betrayed. I felt abandoned. I was afraid. I wanted comfort and compassion and someone I could turn to, but that wasn't what I got. My mother's response upset me very much. While using my mind might be fine, I was not ready to hear it phrased that way. I could not handle being called a cripple, especially by my own mother.

She then asked me to admit to her that I was a cripple. When she did not get immediate obedience, she slapped me. But that wasn't enough—she wouldn't relent until I obeyed, so I finally complied and said I was a cripple. It really hurt saying that, and it hurt me even more that I was having to say it to her.

My mother's heartfelt intentions were not coming through in the actions she chose, just as my actions were not clearly communicating to others what was going on inside of me so that the people around me would know how best to help me. No one but me realized that there wasn't anyone there for me. No one was there to talk me through what had just happened. I was confused, upset, angry, and alone. I had never seen an amputee before, and now I was one.

THE TROPHY

We stayed in Chicago for my rehab; and, along with my rehab, I wanted to play sports. My mom had been an athlete, so she was happy to sign me up for sports. I tried skiing. I tried football. I tried baseball. I tried basketball. And nobody stopped me. Anything I wanted to try, I was allowed to try.

My mom wasn't just an athlete—she was a very good athlete. She even had a room that was full of the many trophies she had won throughout her life. Unlike her, I didn't have any trophies, and it bothered me. I very much wanted one.

Just a year after my amputation, I came across an advertisement for a BMX bike competition. I thought to myself, I can compete. I have a bike. It was a Kmart bike that I had customized. It looked much fancier and more expensive than it really was since I had removed the store stickers and replaced them with Mongoose stickers. This was my chance! Surely, my fancy white wheels could carry me to a trophy against the other children in the neighborhood and their fancy bikes. I was ready to be in the BMX competition.

On the day of the race, there was a torrential downpour in Evanston, Illinois. This wasn't just a rainy day—it was horrible. But that didn't deter me. I rode my bike to the high school, where the competition was supposed to be held, but it was raining so hard, no one else showed up. There were no other children there, except me. Everybody else had assumed it was canceled due to the rain. Only the organizers were there, and I could easily see they were going to pack up and leave.

Because my prosthetic leg would absorb water and swell, I wasn't supposed to get it wet. But I didn't care. I wanted to win a trophy. I didn't care about any prize money or other awards, but they mentioned there would be trophies, and that's what I wanted more than anything in the world. I told the organizers my story about my leg and why I wanted a trophy so bad, and one of them said he'd compete against me.

He said, "Okay, we are going to ride bikes as slow as we can and see how long you can go without pedaling. You get to pedal one time, and then we coast and ride as slow as we can and whoever goes the farthest wins."

I think he tried to give me the win, but I still lost.

When it was over, he handed me the second-place trophy. It was the most euphoric, encouraging, positive moment I'd ever experienced. I won something! I didn't care that there were no competitors besides me and the organizer, although I do like to joke that, in some respects, I came in second to a professional rider. I think they might have also tried to give me something else, but I only wanted the trophy. My laser-focused goal to win a trophy had been achieved, and it was amazing.

I hurried home to show my mom. It was still raining, and I was holding the trophy in my right hand. I knew that if I stood up to pedal, I could go faster, but when I went to stand up and do the fast ride home, I realized I also needed my right hand on the handlebar. But there was one problem—the trophy was in that hand, and there was no way I was letting go of it. Because I didn't have a good grip on the handlebars, I fell off the bike into a gravel pit, but I never let my trophy hit the ground. My forearms were covered with rocks and scrapes, but I didn't care that I was bleeding. The only thing that mattered was that trophy, and I held onto it tightly. It was mine. It was the most monumental and important thing ever. I had earned it. I had won. I had done something that no one thought I could do. And I proudly carried that trophy all the way home.

When I finally arrived home, I was soaking wet and my arms were bleeding, but I was smiling bigger than ever as I held the trophy up in my hand. "Mom, I did it! I got one!"

My little trophy was given its own spot in the trophy room.

For the first time, I felt like I had something to contribute.

HULK HOGAN

Fitness started becoming part of my life at the age of twelve. I was a fan of Hulk Hogan, and my grandma bought me the Hulkamania workout set, complete with blue dumbbells, a headband, and a workout cassette. I wanted to be like the Hulkster, so I would put on my Hulkster t-shirt and work out with the dumbbells. I listened to the cassette tape until I wore it out, and I did everything the Hulkster said I should do. The Hulkster would tell all of us Hulkamaniacs to say our prayers, take our vitamins, and do all the other great things that would help us become good, strong people.

I also loved the WWF wrestler figurines and looked forward to receiving them for holiday presents and rewards for good grades. My mom and grandma would buy the figurines because I loved them, and it was a blessing for them if they happened to be on sale. WWF and the Hulkster were everything to me.

I believed in the Hulkster so much that, at times, my mom and I would get into battles over him.

At one point, Mom decided I was getting a little too caught up in the Hulkamania frenzy. She challenged me to really think about what I was seeing. "Son, do you really believe it is real that someone could take a steel chair and hit you upside the head multiple times, beat you for fifteen minutes, and all it takes is someone saying your name for you to get back up? As if all of a sudden, the steel chair does not hurt anymore? Do you really think that is possible?"

I would respond with, "If 10,000 Hulkamaniacs are behind you, yes, you can. You can be hit upside the head with a chair and all that and still be okay if 10,000 Hulkamaniacs are behind you."

The Hulkster was why I started lifting weights and working out. He was my hero, so you can imagine the heated argument when she would ask, "Do you really believe that?"

I would get in her face and say, "Yes, if 10,000 Hulkamaniacs are behind you, you can do anything."

She banned me from the Hulkster.

Wrestlemania was coming up, and the Iron Sheik was going to be going up against Hulk Hogan, but Mom had banned me from watching it because I believed wrestling to be real, and I was making an idol out of Hulk Hogan. Despite all her best efforts and logic, she could not convince me that the Hulkster was not real.

This became my entre into public speaking. I put a campaign together to convince my mother to let me watch Wrestlemania. I could not be the one Hulkamaniac who could not support the Hulkster. I rallied the neighborhood kids to come and tell my mother that the Hulkster was going to lose if we did not all watch it together.

My mother already knew me to be one who would resort to verbal persuasion. Any time my behavior warranted discipline, I would always stop my mom first and say, "Let me explain." She was a firm believer in spare the rod, spoil the child, and she was determined that I would not be spoiled. My verbal persuasive attempts did not necessarily work, but I would always try to talk my way out of whoopings. As far as she was concerned, "You go ahead, and as soon as you are done…"

It was a war of wills, and I would try to keep the talking going forever. No matter how hard I tried, though, Mom always won. Mom's philosophy was, in spite of disabilities or anything else, you are still human, and you still have to conduct yourself in a certain way. My behavior was not handicapped, and she wasn't going to treat me like I was handicapped. She had now learned and believed one of the biggest handicaps being put on children was when their parents treated them like they were handicapped.

As the date for Wrestlemania and the match between Hulk Hogan and the Iron Sheik drew closer, it was imperative that I take my verbal persuasion strategy to the next level. As I rallied my supporters, the neighborhood children became convinced that there was no way that the Hulkster was going to win without my seeing him.

"James, the Hulkster needs you." I said, "I know. I know. The Hulk said, 'I am facing the biggest threat to Hulkamaniacs everywhere.' If he does not have every voice, there is no way he can win."

I got the whole neighborhood to come to my house. They were persuaded and moved to action. If we did not see this together, we were convinced that the Hulk would not win.

We absolutely had to convince Mom that I should be allowed to watch Wrestlemania. Unlike back home in Indiana, my neighborhood in Chicago was very diverse. Even with our diversity, we were unified in our mission. The Armenian, Jamaican, African, German, white, and even the Hispanic child who lived next door and could barely speak English came to my house to persuade my mom.

"If we do not do this together, the Hulkster is going to get down at some point, and he may lose."

One of my friends turned on the guilt trip and said, "Mrs. Dixon, you do not want the Hulkster to lose to the Iron Sheik because of you, do you?"

Mom relented, and we were able to watch Wrestlemania together. At one point, the Hulkster was losing, but because we cheered and believed, he came through, even with the referee cheating him.

BACK TO INDIANA

I had progressed with my rehab, and it was no longer as important that we remain in Chicago. That's when I started begging my mom to move back to Indiana. I needed to be closer to Grandma. She had been very involved in my life, and I missed her. When I was younger in Indiana and my mother had to work, she would have me spend time with Grandma. I had spent so much time with her that I created a unique bond with her. Grandma filled a big void in my life. She was my confidant and confidence builder. Grandma was everything to me.

In the neighborhood in Chicago, I saw disabled and challenged children. The acceptance was phenomenal, and it made kids like me forget we had a disability. The other children had accepted me with a disability. They had seen me go from crutches to learning to walk again. They simply accepted me just like I was.

We moved back to Indiana, and for the first time, I was in a circle where people were not accepting. Even though I was born there, the rejection level was high. I didn't know any amputees and had never seen one. There were none in my hometown.

I did not want to be known as the kid with the "wooden leg." I can remember trying to deny it, trying to pretend like it was not wooden, and trying to avoid situations where they could tell. I would try to avoid walking when people could see me walk. I would move with the crowd and try to hide in it. I had even gotten into fights with people trying to prove that I did not have it. No matter how much I tried to find acceptance, I just could not.

One day at school, a student decided to pull a prank. He put a stick into a sock and put a shoe on the end of it. He came onto the bus and showed it to everyone. At lunchtime when the whole school was there, he was going to bring it out. Some of the other students came to me and told me, "Do not say anything to that student because if you say anything, he is going to embarrass you." I had no idea what he was planning, and no one was telling me.

At lunchtime, it was bothering me that everyone was saying, "He is going to embarrass you if you say anything to him," so I asked him, "What is it that you have? What are you going to say about me? What is it that everyone is talking about?"

He said, "Exhibit A," and he pulled out this thing he had made with the stick, the sock, and the shoe and said, "I got your leg." The entire lunchroom erupted in laughter. The students were running out like they had just witnessed the final punch in mortal combat. It was his "you have finished him" moment.

That was probably the most devastating moment I had endured up to that point.

PHYS ED CLASS

With no amputees in my hometown in Indiana, not only had I never seen one until I became one, my peers had never seen one until they saw me. It was new to my teachers, too, and none of them had never worked with an amputee student.

Because I was different, I did everything I could to hide my leg from my classmates. I even failed a physical education class because the instructor wanted me to wear shorts. He did not understand all the reasons for my request for accommodation to wear sweatpants and told me I had to wear shorts to class. If I wore shorts, my fellow students would see my leg, and I knew they would be cruel and hurtful in both actions and words. So I simply could not wear shorts.

A portion of our physical education class involved swimming. I asked the instructor if there was anything I could do instead of swimming. My instructor suggested I take the leg off and swim. He simply could not understand that the leg was part of who I am, and the judgment and cruelty from fellow classmates would be unbearable. The idea of taking the leg off seemed even worse than the shorts, so I swam with the leg on and sweatpants trying to hide it.

These efforts to protect my emotional wellbeing led to physical problems. The leg was not supposed to get wet, and since it did get wet, there were issues with the fit. That led to rubbing, which caused a sore, which led to another surgical revision.

I requested privacy for showering because I didn't want my leg to be seen, but the instructor would not make an allowance for me to shower privately or simply skip the shower altogether. I would simply have to settle for failing physical education, something that seems so ironic in hindsight.

Peer interactions at school were challenging, and I tried to hide behind humor and cracking jokes. I tried to befriend the right people; however, my leg always seemed to be in the way. My leg also became the reason I could not date or keep a girlfriend. If I liked a girl and it looked like there might be mutual attraction, the guys would simply ask her, "Are you going with the dude with one leg?" and she would instantly lose interest.

JORDANS

As a young man, I wanted to dress like my peers, and the brand of sneakers was important to me. On my fourteenth birthday, my mom agreed to buy me a pair of Air Jordans. This was a dream come true. Up until I was eleven, when my leg was amputated, all my shoes were custom made. To compensate for my right leg not growing as fast as my left, my right shoe was always custom made. A standard shoe was built up by adding more and more layers to the bottom, much like a platform shoe. With the prosthetic, I could have a normal pair of shoes and feel a little more like a regular kid. At this age, I could still fit in the Jordans, which only went up to size 13.

My mom had to work, so it was impractical for her to take me to the mall to get them. She and Grandma gave me cash and asked my older cousin to take me. He was a boxer and in his 30s, so he was definitely capable of assisting with the purchase and keeping me out of trouble. He was supposed to take me to the mall, get the shoes, and return me home.

As we headed out to his car, he asked me, "How old are you?" I confirmed that I was fourteen. He told me, "You are a man now." I asked, "What?" He proceeded to educate me, "Yes, at fourteen, you are grown." I was rather intrigued by this, "Wow! I did not know that."

We went to the mall, and I picked out the Jordans. They were the Black Metallic Jordan 5s with the red Michael signature on the silver tongue. They were the coolest sneakers.

I had some money left over after paying for the shoes, and my cousin asked, "What are you going to do with that extra money?" I had not really thought about it and responded, "I don't know." He was ready with a plan and suggested, "Let's go get you a girl."

I was taken aback, "What?"

He drove us to the next city, and he told me to tell the girl that I am 18. I had just turned 14, and there was no way I could pass for 18. When she went to ask my name, I blurted out, "I am 18." Now, she had kids. She knew I was lying. She knew I was not 18.

We went to a hotel, and my cousin got a room for him and his girl. He suggested I go get a room with my girl. All I could think was, "No, I don't want to do that." It was a big enough deal that I now had a girlfriend, or so I was convincing myself. Granted, I did not know this girl. I had just met her, but the fact that she was with me made her my first girlfriend. She was being nice to me, so I thought, "I love her." The fact that she had kids seemed to be an afterthought.

My cousin eventually came out, and he was convinced I had

squandered an opportunity and wasted my money. I was elated because when I asked if she would be my girlfriend, she said, "Yeah." My fourteen-year-old brain was speeding all the way to the next day at school. Oh! My goodness, I couldn't wait to get to school so I could tell my best friend and all the fellas, "I got a girlfriend. I finally got one."

While we were off on the Air Jordan and "girlfriend" adventure, Mom was at work. Her shift ended at 11 p.m., and I was supposed to have been home before 9:00. It was now almost midnight. I knew she had to be home, and she had likely realized that I was not there. When we pulled up to the house, it was obvious that she was up and worrying because all the lights in the house were on.

On the drive from the hotel to my house, my cousin coached me about how to handle Mom. He was reinforcing the idea that I was now a man. I was excited. I now had my Jordans. I now had a girlfriend with two kids. I was the man.

My cousin told me, "You have got to just tell your mom you are a grown man now. You are going to respect her, as long as she respects you."

I rehearsed my lines in the car, and I was ready when I entered the door. Meanwhile, my cousin took off down the road. I had wanted him to come in with me, but he said, "No. You gotta do this yourself. You are a man."

I was used to being a latchkey kid, so I opened the door with my key and entered. As expected, my mom was sitting in her chair waiting for me. I said, "Eloise…" This was the first time in my life I had ever called her by her first name, so some of you are probably wondering how I lived long enough to write this book.

Mom had presumed we went to the movies and asked me where I had been. Still extremely confident in my newfound manhood, I said, "I am glad you asked me that. In fact, I am glad you are up because if you were not up, I was going to wake you up." I proceeded to explain to her how I am a grown man and parroted the lines of my cousin, "I will respect you if you respect me. I will come in when I want and leave when I want."

I was so oblivious in my confidence, or perhaps more accurately stated, cockiness, that I did not realize she had gotten up from her seat and was approaching me. I was in the middle of my speech, and she interrupted it. In my naivety, I presumed she would take this news like a calm and rational adult. I drastically underestimated Mom in this moment, and let's just say one of the chairs in the house did not fare well in the exchange. Mom went next level.

I may have been taller than her since the fourth grade, but she was still Mom and would not be intimidated. She worked very hard and was attempting to treat me like any normal child by surrounding me with love and discipline. She was a single parent, and she needed to show me what being a man meant. Men have to accept the consequences of their actions, and she was all too happy to give me that lesson.

The consequences for me included taking back the Jordans. She also layered on more chores. Her third punishment was to take away my prosthetic. I was allowed to borrow it from her for school; but, after school, I had to turn it back in. It was like my leg was a rental, and she controlled the terms of the arrangement. After school, my friends would ask me to come outside, but I could not tell them about my leg punishment, so I would say, "No. I'm gonna just stay inside. I'll talk through the window. No, go home. I'll call you on the phone. We'll be friends on the phone."

Mom may have been slight in stature compared to me, but she was a formidable opponent.

MY FATHER

Mom had seen and experienced what happens when a young man thinks he is a "man" long before he really is. She did not want to see me repeat some of my father's unhealthy behavior patterns.

My parents married in their late teens, and I soon arrived on the scene. Mom was focused on doing the best she could to care for me, and Dad was free to do what he wanted to do. He struggled with the reality that his child had a disability. Sometimes he came to doctors' appointments if he was needed for a signature for permission to operate, but, otherwise, he left most of the responsibility to Mom. She often had to plead with him to step in if she could not get off work for an appointment. One time, she became very frustrated because the hospital sent him home. At first, she thought it might have been an issue relating to skin color, but then she learned he was not sensitive to hospital protocol around preventing additional sickness for already sick children. For the safety of the medically-fragile children, he was told to leave.

When we started working with Shriners, my father was not really involved and was not living with us. My mother was able to convince him to go to the hospital because the Shriners took care of everything. All he had to do was ride up and be a parent. The Shriners provided transportation and paid for everything. They even fed him while he was there at the hospital with me. I remember that he took full advantage of the free food.

There were times when I was growing up when my dad would call and say he was coming to pick me up or was on his way over to see me. I wanted to be visible to him when he drove up the main street and would sit on the steps leading up to the porch. I didn't want him to drive by and potentially miss me. Sometimes I would be out there for hours waiting, and he would not come. I remember after a while my mother would come out and try to coax me to come back inside. She had a difficult time because I was afraid if I went inside, he might drive by and miss me. What if he came, and I was not there? Would he just drive away, thinking I didn't want to see him? All too often, his promises of visits went unfulfilled. I would be devastated, but in the process of being let down, I learned the coping skills of self-soothing.

When we returned to Indiana after my time at Shriners and living in Chicago, I would see my dad periodically; but he was not the type to get actively involved. Still, my mother never spoke ill of him. She was never negative. As far as she was concerned, his relationship with me was his responsibility, and she was not going to interfere with that either way. When I did see him, I was respectful, which was not only expected, but required. I never questioned him. I simply learned that this was just the way Dad was.

As an adult, my relationship with my father is much better. There has been forgiveness and reconciliation. I know he has regrets and remorse for things that happened in my childhood. In my forties, he has been making up for lost time. For my birthday, he will hand deliver a card, and he has given me a bracelet. He is not a man of many words, but I know his heart is in the right place. The interaction might be little more than a knock on the door and a short conversation of "I was just driving by. Happy Birthday, Son. Love you." The gift of his appearance means a great deal to me and allows me to forgive all the time he was absent. I have moved beyond the need to ask "Why?" for everything in the past and am content to build our relationship now.

One day when I was working at a church building and my boys were with me, my dad stopped by so we could all take a photo together. I looked down and noticed his shoes were a little worn. I asked, "What size shoes do you wear?" He said 15. It was a bit of a "wow" moment for me because I really didn't know that many things about him. Since I also wore size 15, I took the shoes off my feet and gave them to him. As a fitness clothing model, I am often sent extra pairs of shoes. Sometimes it is great to be able to grab a pair of my expensive dress shoes and bless him with them.

I do not know the challenges my father faced throughout his life and have chosen to give him grace. I remember when my father used alcohol as a crutch. I remember him being a great guy when sober, and alcohol would change that. Alcohol can rob a person of their purpose. For that very reason, I have chosen to stay away from alcohol. My father has found the Lord, and his brother is a pastor. Fortunately, when I was growing up, I had uncles who were tremendous role models and helped to fill in the gap of the father figure I needed. The Bible says God is the father to the fatherless (Psalm 68:5). It is not just God acting as the father but also Him providing men to fill in with different aspects of my life so that my mom never had to be both parents. Mom got to be Mom. Grandma got to be Grandma. Everyone else filled in the gaps.

SIBLINGS

A round the age of eight or nine, I met another boy and discovered he was my half-brother.

When I was fifteen, my cousins and I learned about 900 numbers from the television. Sometimes when lots of my grandma's other grandchildren would come over, I would pick up the phone and call the 900 numbers because the TV said if I called, there were girls waiting to meet me. In my head, these girls were waiting to meet ME, but with everyone there, Grandma would not know who made the phone call. I would drop my voice down low in an attempt to sound older and call, agreeing to the three-dollar connection fee and additional two dollars a minute. We boys could easily spend an hour on the phone, with everyone wanting to take a turn. Sometimes the recording would come on and say, "For ten dollars, there is a girl who wants to meet you locally." To me, that sounded like a good idea, so I dialed the number on the rotary phone.

On this particular day, I was connected to a girl who lived 30 minutes away. I told her I had my own house and cars, which was obviously a lie since I was only 15 at the time. Apparently, it all sounded impressive enough to her that she was willing to meet me in person. We arranged for her to come to my house one day around 2:30 or 3:00 because I knew Mom would be at work at that time.

Finally, the day this young lady was supposed to visit had arrived, and I was excited. I was behaving a little too far outside of my normal character, which had Mom wondering what I was up to. I had been ambitiously cleaning the house, and my mom was taking notice. Trying to figure out if I would divulge my true motives, she said, "Hmm, you are being awful helpful around here. I better take off today."

Of course, I didn't want her to do that and innocently suggested, "No, no, you should go to work. Actually, you should go early. Yes, I'm good. I just want to surprise you." She was growing more suspicious by the minute, and rightly so since I smelled of cologne and was heavily engaged in this out-of-character cleaning spree through the house. Well, Mom's intuition had kicked in, and she knew I was up to something. She decided she would stick around.

Time was not in my favor at this point, and all I could think was "She has gotta leave." Alarms were now going off in her head because I was trying everything to get her to go. I was all but begging her. I kept trying different persuasive tactics, "Go to work. You should go now; seriously, you should. There is no reason for you to be here. Take off."

She did not do it.

When the girl knocked on the door, Mom asked, "Who is that?" I attempted to convince her the person must be at the wrong house and headed out to try to get the girl to leave. Obviously, my plan had unraveled.

The girl had an overnight bag with her. Apparently, her parents had not set rules for her. I had never met her before, so how was I going to explain to Mom that I met her by calling a 900 number? How was I going to get her out of there before Mom really started figuring things out?

Now seemed like as good a time as any to start telling the truth, so I looked at the girl and said, "Okay. Listen. I do not have a house. I do not have a car or anything. I still live with my parents." And she said, "Yeah, I know that. We are fifteen." I had to step up the truth message and said, "I was lying. I am saying you gotta go." She responded, "No, I had them drop me off. I live over a half hour away." I was now ready to try anything. "Maybe we can get you a Greyhound bus ticket to go back home or something." I was more than ready to look up the Greyhound schedules—whatever it took to get her out of there before Mom caught on.

My mom decided it would be a good time to join in the conversation and asked, "Who is this young lady?" Before I could open my mouth, the girl said, "I came to spend some time with James." *Oh, boy*, I thought. Mom questioningly responded, "Oh, really!?" The girl then added, "I was going to spend the night."

Things had gone from bad to worse, and I needed this girl to stop talking. She was getting me in so much trouble.

Mom was now quite interested in this little mess I had gotten myself into. I knew she was not liking this young lady's plan to spend the night, but she was all too happy to let this young lady keep talking. She was collecting lots of information, which would definitely be used against me later. In my mind, I thought, *this is horrible; I'm busted*. My mom then asked, "Who are your parents?" The girl gave her mom's name and then said, "My dad's name is Elmer."

Could it really be that I had just met my half-sister through a 900 number, and my first girlfriend might have been my half-sister if mom had not been there? I was in shock. I have a sister!?

I asked, "How old are you?" She confirmed, "Fifteen." To which I said, "But I'm fifteen." I thought to myself that she had to be making this up because her birthday was less than three weeks from mine. My dad said he had never cheated when he was married to my mom, but the fact that I had met a half-brother several years earlier meant that was untrue. If this was truly my half-sister, then there wasn't a shadow of a doubt that his words weren't true.

We climbed into Mom's car and headed to Dad's house. I had never spent the night at his place, and on the rare occasion that I went to his house, I would always knock and wait for him to let me in. When we arrived at the house, she just walked right in the front door and said, "Heah, Daddy" to which he responded "Heah, Baby." At this point I realized he definitely did know her, and it was confirmed she was my half-sister.

Sometime later, my half-brother and I were riding bicycles elsewhere in the neighborhood and came across another fifteen year old, who also turned out to be a half-sister. She was just a week younger than me. Dad might have been married to my mom, but apparently as he was just a teenager, he had not yet settled down into the idea of singular commitment. He had managed to have four children, two boys and two girls, all within one year, with three of the children having been born within three weeks of each other.

Obviously, Dad was too busy with other things to be attentive to me in those early years of my life.

Fortunately, all of us siblings found our way through our challenged starts to much more productive adult lives. Sadly, we lost my half-brother to gun violence; however, he had accepted Christ, so I have the promise that I will see him again in Heaven someday.

BASKETBALL

As I entered my freshman year of high school, I noticed that basketball was how everyone was getting acknowledgment and recognition in Indiana, so I wanted to play and decided I would try out for the high school team. I had been playing basketball, so it was not new to me. I had played against adults and had learned that if I played with aggression, I could overcome some of my limitations in mobility.

Playing was not new, but playing as part of an organized team would be new. The tryouts came, and I was confident I could make the team. I had played in the open gym against several of the other students aspiring to join the team and knew that I was better than quite a few. While I was a freshman, I had gone through a growth spurt, so I was over 6 feet tall. In my opinion, there was no reason why I would not make the team. I could shoot with either hand. I could play defense and rebound. I was strong. There was no question about it—I was going to make the team.

The coach began the tryouts with a one-mile run. He announced, "You have to run it within five minutes and ten seconds. If you can't, you are cut." I had never done that before, and I was not prepared.

The second test was to run while doing lots of lateral moves. This was another thing I had not anticipated, and I was not prepared. We never did get around to demonstrating what I considered basketball skills on that first day of the tryouts.

Following the first day, the coach posted the list of who made the team and who did not. He posted it before the school day finished and then left. There would be no one there to address any questions. I couldn't wait to see if my name was on the list. I knew I would have to call Mom to come pick me up from school after practice, so I ran outside to see if I made the team. I checked and double checked the list. Everyone made the team, except for me.

I ran my finger up and down the list, hunting for my name. Realizing that my name was not on the list was a significant moment. Earlier that year, I had learned about another list where I wanted my name to be included. It was the list of names in the Lamb's Book of Life.

16

HEAVEN'S GATES AND HELL'S FLAMES

One of the teachers in the public school I was attending was a Christian. I had been struggling in her class and needed all the extra credit I could get to maintain the grades necessary to keep academic eligibility for sports. She promised extra credit if I went to a play at her church. The play was entitled "Heaven's Gates and Hell's Flames."

I rode with my teacher to the play and sat in the very back because it was an all-white church, and as I saw it, I was the only cool person among the few hundred people in the building. I was especially cool in my Bull's starter jacket. As I looked around the room, I didn't see anyone I knew. The truth is I didn't want anyone to know I was in the church with her out of fear that they'd think I was kissing up or brown nosing.

The one-hour play opened with a dramatization of the crucifixion of Christ, His battle with Satan, His rising again from the dead, and finally His ascension into Heaven. The story included excerpts from popular songs of the time, including the Via Dolorosa, made popular by Sandy Patti, Rise Again with Dallas Holm, and He's Alive by Don Francisco. It also included classics like The Hallelujah Chorus. The play was a sequence of everyday skits with everyday people who die and find themselves at the Gates of Heaven. The only way they can enter is if their name is in the Lamb's Book of Life. Either they are welcomed into Heaven by Jesus, or they are taken to Hell by Satan and his demons. The skits could change from show to show, but the common theme was they were relatable to the people in the audience and communicated the consistent message that whether you make it into Heaven comes down to your personal decision to accept Jesus' free gift of salvation.

One skit might show the kind old grandmother who lived a life of service and is welcomed into Heaven. The next might show the partying teens and pastor's son who find they are taken to Hell because they never made a personal decision to accept Christ. That scene could be followed by the family with a son who accepted Christ at church that morning, and everyone is welcomed into Heaven and reunited with a young family member who died years earlier. In contrast, the next could be the father and son who had time for sports and material things, but erroneously thought there was plenty of time and mom's faithfulness to her church would somehow cover them. That could be followed by a who keeps promising to go to church with her daughter, only to find as they arrive at the gates that mom is whisked away to Hell and the daughter enters Heaven without her. Another scene might show a woman who feels betrayed by her husband and ends her life only to find that there really is life after death and because she never accepted Christ, she is now going to Hell. The message that time is of the essence might be driven home with a skit depicting two construction workers talking over lunch, and the conversation leads to one choosing to accept Christ and then, moments later, an accident brings them to Heaven's Gates, where he finds that his name is among the newest entries in the Lamb's Book of Life.

I specifically remember a skit with a businessman who died and arrived at the Gates of Heaven. He was asked, "Why should I let you in?" His answer was "I have made a lot of money, have given to a lot of causes, and have done a lot of wonderful things." He was told, "You did not mention one thing that mattered. What did you do with Jesus?" He responded, "Well, my good days outnumbered my bad days, right?" Heaven's gatekeeper said, "All your good and all your righteousness is but filthy rags. As good as you are, the standard is Jesus. If you did not do what He did or accept Him doing it for you, how are you going to get in? The gulph between you and Him is too big because of sin."

I also remember a plane crash scene, and it was particularly impactful when the demons came up and took a lady down to Hell. I realized the people who got into Heaven got in because of Jesus and accepting Him as their Savior.

The pastor gave an invitation for salvation. I do not recall walking forward; all I know is one moment I was in the back row uninterested, and then, all of a sudden, I was at the altar for the altar call.

My reason for going forward to the altar wasn't because I didn't want to go to Hell. I went forward because I felt that God loved ME, and for the first time in my life, I knew it. All the feelings I had my whole life of not being accepted and loved were rising up in my heart and being covered by His love. It was so genuine. He loved

ME! All the fronting and pretending I was doing to hide the pain inside did not matter to Him. He loved ME! All the pretending I was doing trying to be more than I was as an athlete did not matter to Him. He loved ME! All the strong man images I was creating about myself did not matter to Him. He loved ME!

For the first time, I realized leg or no leg, God loved ME! It didn't matter that I was an amputee. He loved ME! This was the same God that Grandma talked to me about over all those years. Grandma used to say, "God has no grandchildren." I had to know Him for myself. Her faith would not save me. Mom's faith would not save me. Here in this little church at that altar, faith was real to ME. I knew I needed Him, and I wanted Him for ME. There was no family there. There was nobody watching. There was no sense of shame. All I knew was I wanted to be saved.

Counselors came forward, gathering people to pray with, and I didn't want to be left out. I remember grabbing a guy and saying, "I want to be saved." He tried to take me to one of the side rooms, but they were all packed. He took me outside under a streetlamp because it was the only place that we could get enough light so that he could see his Bible to take me through the scriptures of the "Roman's road." He explained the plan of salvation to me, and it was there that I accepted Christ.

I immediately felt so different. A burden had been lifted. I was excited and tearful all at the same time. I realized God loves ME! He loves ME! He loves me more than my biological father has ever loved me. He loves me more than Mom. He loves me more than Grandma. He loves ME! It didn't matter how many times I had messed up or how I felt about myself. He loves ME!

That public school teacher probably had no idea how impactful that moment was going to be. For her, it was a passive evangelism moment to invite me, but for me, it would change the entire trajectory of my life. God's acceptance and love of me was all encompassing and accomplished all. It was whole and pure. Despite all my struggling and all I had done, He still accepted me.

When my teacher took me back to my home, the new me was elated and ecstatic. I was bouncing off the wall. God loves me! The realization of His love had just filled a void in me. Grandma loved me, and she loved me completely to the core. I knew Mom loved me, but to truly feel that God loved me was medicine to the soul. I had been so sick and sad inside because of my sin, but now my sins were forgiven.

I had become quite a challenge for my mom. In my efforts to try to be popular, I had made poor decision after poor decision. I had taken her car and wrecked it. I had caused her so much pain and frustration that I remember when Magic Johnson made the announcement on TV that he was retiring from the NBA because he had HIV, she said to me, "I would rather you had it than Magic Johnson." I didn't know how to take that. "Well, you are not doing anything with your life," she explained.

At the time, I was just a teenager, but, on some level, she was right. My sins were taking me down a very bad path. Mom didn't care how I felt about what she said, but she hoped that I would do something in response to her words. Her philosophy was, if you want me to feel differently, then show me different.

She had her own brand of tough love. I was a boy and, therefore, she had to be tough on me. She knew I was a black child with a disability, and nobody was going to take it easy on me, so she would not. While it was hurtful, in hindsight, I am appreciative of all the tough lessons. The lessons did not affect her love for me or whether I felt loved. Her words were chosen for their shock and awe effect.

With Jesus now in my heart, I no longer wanted to continue down the self-destructive path of making bad decisions. I immediately realized that I wanted to obey God in thanks for the overwhelming love He has for me. His love was washing away years of pain that was hidden in my heart.

My grandma and mom hadn't gone to school with me and heard all the remarks I was subjected to. They were not with me when kids made fun of me. They didn't know that I had a regimen of sitting in my room trying to create ankles for my prosthetic and attempting to make them thick enough so people could not tell. They did not see when my shoe would curl up on one side because the prosthetic was not big enough. They weren't there when I was trying to get rid of the line at the kneecap. They did not know all the pain inside that God's love had just covered and healed in an instant.

17

A NEW ME

I was radically changed.

The night I got saved, I went home and knew I needed to get rid of all the rap CDs and pornographic magazines I had hidden in my room. But I knew I couldn't just give all the things away. I had to make sure they were destroyed and thus could not become part of someone else's sins. I couldn't sleep that night without getting rid of all of it, but I also couldn't just leave it in the trash can inside the house. So, I grabbed all the stuff and went across the street and found a dumpster and proceeded to physically destroy and tear the stuff up as I threw it away. No one told me to do that. Somehow, the conviction in my heart was so strong it compelled me to act. The moment I got rid of it, I remember feeling so clean and different.

The joy of knowing my name was in the Lamb's Book of Life was beyond explanation. I was so excited I couldn't sleep. "I am saved because of what Jesus did. I am saved." Just knowing that was amazing, but I was hungry to learn more.

I had a long history of reading the Bible, but now I was different. From a young age, I would often read the Bible out loud to Grandma in the kitchen, and she would explain to me what I had read. At times, Grandma had boarders staying with her. They were generally older people who had no family, and she would have me read the Bible to them, also. I had developed confidence in reading out loud and, at times, would read in church. I remember Mom always said it didn't matter if you went somewhere on Saturday, you still had to get up for church on Sunday. Even with that solid background in faith, it was not until I walked down that aisle and accepted Jesus for myself that my passion for Bible reading and church attendance became real.

When I was growing up, there was always a Bible sitting on the back of the toilet. It was the Living Bible. It sounds a little humorous, but with my newfound passion to read the Bible, it was not uncommon for me to spend more time in the bathroom than usual, simply reading and studying the Bible. The bathroom became a place of spiritual growth for me.

Sunday came around, and no one came from that church to pick me up to take me to services, so I made a phone call. A gentleman answered the phone and told me to find a church near where I lived. I started calling around and telling them, "I am looking for a Bible-believing church where I can learn," because that was what the guy told me to find. I was reading the Bible, and I wanted someone to explain to me what I was reading.

I didn't even own a Bible of my own; so, when I saw a commercial for the Seventh Day Adventists, I called them and said, "I need a Bible." Some Mormons from the Church of Jesus Christ of Latter-

Day Saints came to my door, but I rejected them because they were saying stuff I could not agree with. What they were saying was not lining up with my interpretation of what I was reading in my Bible.

I may have just been a teenager, but I was determined to find a church. I eventually called Grace Baptist Church and spoke to Pastor Leigh Crockett. Pastor Crockett was a distant relative of American explorer Davy Crockett, and he personally came and picked me up. It was a large church, but he obviously sensed my sincere hunger to learn. I was so on fire for the Lord, and he was always willing to explain things to me and answer my questions. It was one of those more traditional churches, where people do not talk much or say amen much during sermons.

While others weren't too vocal, everything in me wanted to react to his preaching. He would explain something, and my internal reaction would be, "Wow! Man, that was good. Wow! I did not see that coming." He was an expository preacher, and I appreciated how he explained the meaning of the passages of Scripture.

I was there on Sundays and Wednesday nights. At the end of the services, there were tapes of the sermon, and I would get them so I could listen to them during the week to glean everything I could out of the sermon. I was so hungry that I would ask the person at the counter for any other tapes they might have, perhaps sermons from last year. "Got any more tapes? What about last year? Got some of last year's tapes?" I would go home, and after putting them in my Walkman audio player, I would experience even more. "Wow, did not expect that!" While I thoroughly enjoyed listening to the tapes, they weren't entertainment for me. They were another component of genuine discipleship.

The years of learning the art of persuasion took on an eternal significance. I had transitioned from the days of persuading for Hulkamania to persuading people to give me an opportunity to prove myself. I was beginning to overcome the need for people to validate me because now I had found validation in Christ. The young people who called me friend, those who called me crippled, and even those who tortured me and made moments of my childhood nearly suicidal, I now saw through new eyes. They needed Christ just as much as I did.

Now that I had accepted Christ, I wanted everyone to know about Him and started taking others to church with me. My charisma and persuasive skills led me to reach out to Pastor Crockett again. With other people joining me, there were too many people for Pastor Crockett to pick up by himself. We needed something bigger, so the church started sending a van out to get me and everyone I wanted to bring along. I quickly filled the van, and then I asked for the first three rows at church. I was the only minority in that church, but that didn't bother me. Everyone needed Jesus, and that had nothing to do with skin color. I graduated to a bus and rapidly filled those first three rows. Some of the young people who came to Christ in that season have become lifelong friends, even some of the kids who had been cruel to me.

Finding Christ and becoming passionate about reading the Bible also filled another void. As I was reading the Old Testament, I came across a character in 2 Samuel to whom I could relate. That's when I realized there was a kid in the Bible like me. Mephibosheth was the son of Jonathan and the grandson of King Saul. His father, Jonathan, was killed in battle when he was young. A nurse was hastily fleeing to protect him, but she dropped him, causing both of his feet to become crippled. He considered himself to be but a dead dog, and I could relate to that feeling because that summed up my feelings about my life. I believed I had no use. I had no acceptance. No matter what potential I would have had, it was gone because of what I had lost. I could relate to Mephibosheth because I, too, was lame on my feet through no fault of my own.

King David remembered his friend, Jonathan, and brought Mephibosheth to his house. The crippled kid got to sit at the king's table. King David was like the role of Christ in my life. He put Mephibosheth at the same table and said you will eat at my table continually. King David gave him leadership and gave him the land that his grandfather, Saul, tried to fight to maintain. Just as King David saw past Mephibosheth's disability, God can see past mine. Just as it took time for Mephibosheth to become an overcomer, it would take time for me, but the seed had been planted. God can take every weakness and turn it into an opportunity for you to be used of Him. Your greatest weakness becomes the strength that He uses. He exalts you so He can be glorified. You are proof that God is real.

> "In the same way, let your light shine before others, that they may see your good deeds and glorify your Father in heaven."
>
> (Matthew 5:16)

ANOTHER RUN AT BASKETBALL

When I did not make the list for the basketball team in my freshman year, I felt embarrassed and angry. I redirected that anger into action. Every morning, I did every training exercise they used to cut me from the team. I got up without an alarm clock, something that started when I got up with my grandma every morning. She would have her coffee, and I would have oatmeal. She had quite the sense of humor. One day I asked, "Grandma, can I have some coffee?" She responded, "Oh Baby, you do not want to drink coffee. It will make you black." I realized, "Oh yeah, I do not want to do that." Somehow, I didn't seem to realize I was already black.

I never did try the coffee, but I would get up and go outside to run. There was a sign outside that advertised that there was a McDonald's one mile away, so I would run the mile between the billboard and the McDonald's. I knew I needed to be under five minutes, so I timed my runs.

I created an exercise regimen from carefully studying the footwork of the basketball players I would watch on TV. Watching the NBA and college championship teams, I studied the players who played on the inside, paying close attention to their legs and how their feet moved. To be successful, I would have to do what they were doing.

My mom bought me a trampoline, and I'd bounce on that trampoline as I watched the games, building endurance while I imagined I was dunking. I had achieved my first dunking success when I was in the eighth grade.

As I approached my sophomore year, I once again believed I would make the team. I was going to make the team, no matter what they said and no matter what they did because to me it wasn't just about making the team—it was about removing the "crippled" label. My leg was not going to hold me back. This time, I was prepared. I had been lifting weights over the previous year. I'd watched Rocky and drank raw eggs. It was nasty, but I was willing to do anything and everything that might give me the edge I needed to be successful. I had long since worn out the Hulk Hogan cassette, but all those pieces of inspiration were now embedded in my DNA. I was embodying everything I had listened to and was going after my all-consuming goal to make the team.

The time came for me to go against the players who had made it the year before. I was unable to separate the feelings I had about their making it and feeling like they were holding me back. I really felt like they were my enemies and couldn't be friendly. They had taken for granted the opportunity that I hadn't gotten.

Before the tryouts in my sophomore year, I went to the athletic director and requested a favor. "Please make sure they give me a fair opportunity. That is all I am asking for. I don't want anything special, but I also do not want the coach to cut me without giving me a chance." Some people had suggested that the coach was racist so there were rumors and innuendos being passed around. Here in Indiana, I had faced the "n" word multiple times by then, but I couldn't speak to whether the coach was judging me based on race. So, I pleaded with the athletic director, who was in authority over the coach, to make sure I wouldn't be unfairly treated. "Please make sure the coach gives me a fair opportunity. Please, if you come in, just make sure he gives me a fair opportunity."

On the first day of tryouts, the coach did the running drills just like he did the year before. Last year, he got rid of me with those, but this time I was not going down. The other guys had done the drills during their seasonal conditioning, but I had done them every day for the entire year. What they did to get in shape, I did as an everyday workout. We were made differently. I thought differently.

We had to run the death valleys or suicides where you touch every line. We would run, touch the line, run, touch the line, etc. It wasn't long before the other players were starting to bend over and throw up. I was not bending over. My hands were on my hips in a defiant Superman stance. I was not going to let him break me. I wanted this more than he knew, and I refused to break. This time, I wasn't the slowest kid, even with one leg and one horrible prosthetic.

In the back of my mind, I knew I was going to pay the price for pushing myself so hard. I was used to struggling to find the right tube socks for my leg that were small enough, smooth enough or whatever to prevent damage to my skin. If I did not plan well, I could tear my skin and then I would not be able to walk. After practices and workouts, I often had to sit in a hot tub with Epsom salts to get rid of boils and infections from the rubbing of my prosthetic.

On this first day of tryouts, no matter how much it hurt or how bad it felt, nothing was going to stop me. We kept running. I was feeling really strong as we entered the final run and was excited because I was going to make it. As I went to turn on the last lap, my kneecap dislocated.

My kneecap dislocated frequently because of this prosthetic. I knew the routine: go to the hospital emergency room, they straighten the leg and pop the knee back in place. There I was in the gym with my knee once again dislocated, knowing the ER trip that awaited me. Yes, I was in physical pain, but the tears running down my face were not due to pain. The tears were because I felt like my dreams were being taken from me again. The athletic director ran out of the room to call for an ambulance, while the other players turned away because it looked gruesome. The coach was trying to console me, saying, "That's alright. You tried. You did good."

When I was preparing for tryouts, I wrote my favorite Bible verse on the back of my shoes. Philippians 4:13 says, "I can do all things through Christ who strengthens me." My real foot was a size fifteen, but my horrible prosthetic was only built to a size nine. As I grew, the prosthetist added vertical inches to the prosthetic, but he did not adjust the foot length to be consistent with my growth. Both of my sneakers were size fifteen, so to make the shoe sort of fit, the shoe on the prosthetic was stuffed with socks. This arrangement was not ideal for my active lifestyle and actually put my knee at risk for frequent dislocation.

So, there I was in the gym with my knee dislocated because my prosthetic had twisted around backwards. The back of my shoe with my favorite Bible verse was now staring me in the face. There was no natural way that should have happened; but, because it did, I had a choice. At that moment, that Bible verse became more than a verse; it was a commandment. "I can do all things. I can get up from this. I can do this." It was time to claim that verse and act on it.

I knew what had to be done, but I had never done this before. Yes, it hurt. Yes, I felt weak; but I got up and pushed my kneecap back into place. I started hopping and then running. As I started running again, I just couldn't stop, even though they were begging me to stop. "There is an ambulance on the way." That didn't deter me—I was not going to stop. I remember the coach trying to stand in front of me and telling me, "No, don't do it. You are hurting yourself." In my head, I was saying, "No, what would have hurt me was to not finish." If I had stopped, it would have meant all the sacrifice and training I'd done all year was for nothing. If I didn't make the team and I gave my best, I could deal with that. But I could not let the leg be what stopped me when I needed this to prove that I was more than my leg.

Unfortunately, I did not make the team; but I would not be counted out just yet.

AAU

I did not make the high school team my sophomore year, so I turned my sights toward the traveling AAU team. Students from all the schools in the area could try out for the team, and they kept only the best. This time, there would be a neutral coach who only wanted the best players. Preferential treatment because of dads and relationships with the coaches would not be an issue.

I had a chip on my shoulder and anger in my chest. The same players who made the high school team over me, the same players who saw me get cut my freshman year and sophomore year, and the same players who saw me get injured and not make it were all going to be competing for positions on the team.

I was now 6'4" and extremely strong. God had given me considerable strength that exceeded that of my peers. If I had wanted to, I could have tossed the other players around; but I would fight them not with fists but with skill and passion on the court. There was a difference between us. I played with playoff intensity, and they played to make a team.

I made that AAU team. I was so excited when I got my jersey that I took it home and slept in it. They had no idea what that meant to me.

I remember when I scored my first basket. On the way home in the van, the other players started chanting about my getting those two points. I was finally being noticed and validated by my peers. Coach Ray Walker, who put me on the team, still plays the video of me talking about how much it meant to me, and it meant everything to me. It didn't matter anymore that I didn't make my high school team. I beat those same players to get on the AAU team. I beat them on a bigger stage. I beat them when there was more competition. It was all because I wanted it more than they did. Some were taller than me. Some had played longer than me, but they did not have the same will and drive.

I remember Grandma coming to a tournament to see me play. I played with tears because I did not want to let her down. I gave everything I had, scoring 20 points and getting 23 rebounds. There was another gear in me. When I played, the disability was something everyone else saw, and I saw validation or the opportunity for it. All I wanted was for someone to say I was enough.

Our team won the state championship for the 17 and under teams.

BENEDICT ARNOLD

My high school struggled with relationships between the races. I had grown up not caring about racial differences because my mother and grandmother never cared about them. We are all made in the image of God; so, as far as I was concerned, differences in skin color did not matter. Unfortunately, not all my peers felt the same way.

One of the young white men in my school was accused of using the "n" word. I didn't believe it could be him because it was not in his nature. I was so sure of it that I was absolutely convinced there was no way he'd said it, but my peers thought otherwise. Some of the students even wanted to beat him up.

One young man who was quite large for his age heard about it and said, "If it only takes saying the 'n' word to get a fight started…" Not surprisingly, he started saying it to our faces, hoping to instigate a fight, one that he would surely win. We would have described him as a country-fed redneck, and he was bigger than some adults. He used his size to his advantage and, sometimes, he used it productively to serve as a bouncer at bars at merely sixteen years of age.

This young man had a reputation. He used to punch himself, head butt lockers, and tear up stuff. No one wanted to fight him. While my peers were ready to fight the small kid who was accused of saying the "n" word, no one was willing to take on this guy. The group waited and finally one day ganged up on the smaller guy. I turned my "friends" into the school authorities, and they started calling me Benedict Arnold. The very kids I had sought acceptance from separated themselves from me.

These kids I had tried to align myself with also had a habit of throwing things at the bus drivers while they were driving us home, which ran off many bus drivers. They would sell and smoke drugs on the bus. It was a bad situation. After those kids separated from me, I didn't sit in the back of the bus with them anymore. Instead, I would sit in the front.

The district hired a little bus driver, a white lady who was under five feet tall and terrified. She announced to the students that she knew the route had a bad reputation, but it was a brand-new bus, and she was going to play whatever radio station they wanted. She was just trying to get along with them, wanting them to be nice. She might as well have just come out and told them to be mean. Just as they had done with all the other bus drivers, they started throwing things at her. I saw that she was so small, so I decided to sit behind her to make sure their projectiles hit me and not her.

She obviously knew where I lived and one day came to my home. My mom saw her at the door and got upset. "James, the school bus driver is here. What have you done?" I honestly responded, "I don't know?" The bus driver had a fruit basket in her hand and addressed my mom, "I want to thank you and thank your son for protecting me." My mother, pleasantly shocked and at a loss for words, replied, "Oh wow, that's great."

The bus driver reported the problem students to the district, and I confirmed what she said. My fellow students were, in fact, throwing things and selling drugs. In the end, my former "friends" were kicked off the bus.

Some of the black parents alleged that this was racism. Once that term entered the conversation, there was pressure to kick the bus driver off the route. There was even a city meeting to discuss getting rid of the white bus drivers on the black side of town.

I was just sixteen, but I went to the meeting. The parents of the drug-dealing students who were trying to get rid of the bus driver, alleging that she had their children kicked off because they were black, sat on one side of the room and, on the other side of the room, all by herself, was the little white lady trying to defend her honor. I sat down beside the bus driver.

I would not sit quietly as community leaders proposed removing her from the black side of town. I stood up and spoke in her defense. I persuaded the leaders not only to keep her, but I convinced them that the other parents were in the wrong.

God had already been preparing me to take stands. Some of the stands were not popular, but I knew I was always supposed to stand up for those who cannot defend themselves or be a voice for those who do not have a voice. Even into adulthood, I have remained in contact with the bus driver and her family, serving them when they need someone to fill a pastoral role.

I learned a great lesson about self-sufficiency and never tried to befriend that group of young people again. They had threatened that they were going to do something to me later, but I was no longer intimidated by them and almost welcomed them to challenge me.

For so long, I had lowered myself to their standard. I had signed up for the same classes as them in order to be accepted. I had done anything and everything in an effort to not be called the one-legged guy. In social settings, I had been afraid to be the first to leave the group because if I did, I was sure they would start talking about me. Interestingly, I would now not even talk to them, and that proved to be advantageous for me. When I separated from them, my grades improved, and I got into honors' classes. I took debate classes and started sharpening my speaking skills. Being distanced from them was not a punishment because I started to thrive. I was doing all these little things without realizing that God was directing my steps. He was separating me from people who I thought I needed for acceptance and validation, and He was guiding me into advocating and ministry.

All I could think about was getting out of high school and moving on. I had not found my identity there—I had found it in Christ. I was growing in confidence as I learned more about God, and I was ready to move on to the next chapter of my life without my former friends. My peers had rejected me as a "Benedict Arnold" for sticking up for someone outside of my race, thus, I didn't want anything to do with any of them. It was during the height of the conflict that they were taking senior pictures at the school, and I chose not to be pictured with them.

At our 30th high school reunion, I realized many of the young people with whom I had so much conflict all those years ago had passed away. Sadly, even at the reunion, there was still a divide between the races. From my perspective, the issues were more about power and control; but racism is an easy excuse for the behavior. By that time, I knew that racism is not a race issue. It is a character issue!

While some classmates might not have changed over the years since high school, others did. I remember there were kids in high school who would punch me or beat on me because I was an easy target. It hurt to have my peers treat me like that and then to have others gather around and laugh as if it were somehow funny. When I encountered one of those classmates later in life, and after noticing that he had not grown since high school, a part of me wanted some revenge. "Thank you, Lord, for delivering him into my hands so I can even the score."

In God's infinitely creative way of teaching me lessons, the man began to share about the hard times he had gone through, how he had been watching me in ministry, and how my words had gotten him through really tough times of loss. "Really, Lord, I guess I have to let that one go."

How many times have I taken advantage of God's grace and mercy in my life? Turning around and giving that man grace and mercy was ultimately more satisfying than if I had gotten revenge. As much as it was wrong of him to attack me when I was defenseless, attacking him from my size now would have made me the bully. He didn't call me an amputee, cripple, wooden leg, fake leg, or all the names the kids had called me in the past. He called me minister and pastor. My selfish human side wished he would have said, "Remember that time..." and then it would have been "ding, round one." It would not have been pretty. I remember having visions and dreams of what I was going to do to that guy, but God had decided it was time for a lesson in forgiveness and compassion. "Lord, You have some humor."

I experienced so much sadness and loneliness in childhood; however, I realize now in hindsight that God might separate you out of the crowd so He can work on you one on one to prepare you to one day lead the crowd. When being left out, alone, or isolated, it might feel like abandonment, but it might also be that you are being prepared to be elevated. Sure, I might have been envious of the popular students when I was 18, but not today, some 30 years later.

SENIOR YEAR

I really wanted to go to college; but, to make that a reality, I was going to need a scholarship. I was determined to do whatever it took to put myself in the best possible position to get that much-needed scholarship.

I had been clipping newspaper articles from my AAU games and sending them to colleges in an attempt to get an athletic scholarship. Knowing I wanted to go somewhere far away because I wanted to be around a new group of people, I went to the library to research schools. For some reason, I decided to look up Minnesota and Bible college.

I wanted to learn more about God because those sessions in the bathroom had become a private sanctuary. I was hungry for more knowledge and understanding. I found a 1-800 number for Pillsbury Baptist Bible College and decided to call them. The woman who answered the phone asked me, "How do you know you are a Christian?" I answered the question as best I knew how; and, apparently, I did well because she said, "That's great." She informed me that my pastor would need to write a letter of recommendation, so I made that a priority. I was officially applying to college.

At the end of our senior year, it was customary to announce students who were being awarded scholarships for various schools. Our town had quite a reputation for basketball, and in my high school years, the number one and number two teams in the nation were right there. There were guys who were 6' 11", 6' 10", and lots of 6' 7" players. I almost seemed short at 6' 4". Only the very best players on our team would get the most coveted scholarships to go on to D1 schools. There were only three students who received scholarships to play basketball. There was a sense of pride and justice as they announced that I had gotten one of only three basketball scholarships awarded to a senior in my class. The very thing every high school basketball player wanted I had actually gotten, even without being accepted by the high school team.

COLLEGE

There I was starting Bible college and having no idea what I was getting into. I was simply excited because I would be learning the Bible.

In college, racism reared its ugly head again. This school was almost entirely made up of white students who came from primarily white communities. Their perception of black people was heavily influenced by what they had read in the paper or heard on TV. I was the first black person many of them had ever met.

My first night on campus, my roommate, whom I had just met and whom I am still great friends with today, said, "My parents want to ask you something." Suspecting nothing, I said, "Sure, what?" He relayed the question, "Do you have a criminal record?" I quickly responded, "No. You cannot even get in here with one." That seemed at face value to satiate that curiosity.

He said, "Okay, one second." He put money on the table and left the room. I was occupied with other things and only marginally paying attention. He came back with a couple of his friends. They counted the money and left. I figured they were trying to gather up money for a pizza, so I put $5 on the table. The guys came back to the room, and they counted it again. Now they were thrown off. I had no idea that they were testing me to see if I would steal the money because they had heard that blacks steal.

There were times in college when I still struggled with acceptance. One day, a fellow student came to me with an idea for a prank. He said, "What if we recorded you being fouled, your leg comes off, and the ref yells, 'That's definitely a foul.'" This was long before the days of social media, and they just thought it would be a fun skit to show in the auditorium. Though I had some reservations, I remember agreeing to it. This was Bible college, and these students meant it for fun, not harm. The child who lost his leg at 11 was still in me and wanted acceptance. Going along with the skit felt like acceptance.

After we did the skit, I remember one of them saying to me, "I thought this would feel funny, but it doesn't." Even though I tried to fake a smile, I could not. Doing something to entertain other people that was not authentic was not for me. One-legged jokes were not funny. The wounds had risen back to the surface; and, unfortunately, for this guy, he would feel more than his fair share of my pent-up aggression. At the Bible college, if you had a dispute with another person, you had the option to go to the individual and talk to him or you could go to the boxing ring in the basement. I invited him down to the boxing ring, where I would set the tone. I went Mike Tyson on Bambi. I was a little too cruel. Even though he was older and my size, he was the embodiment of everyone who had ever voiced a slur about being crippled. After that night, I never had another problem with anyone bringing up the leg again.

My fellow students had come from cultures that were very different from mine, and sometimes it made for some interesting misunderstandings. Sometimes there were things that were common to them that I just did not know. One day, they asked me, "Do you want to go hunting with us?" I had never been hunting, so I said, "Sure." Recognizing I was new to this, they made sure to warn me not to wear cologne because the scent would be picked up by the animals and would mess up the hunt.

As we were getting into the car to go, I asked, "What type of hunting are we doing?" They matter-of-factly said, "We are going coon hunting." Well, where I am from, that meant something different; so, I quickly got out of the car. I said, "No, no. You are not going to shoot me, nah." I was looking at them funny as they were trying to explain to me that they were talking about raccoons. I could not get the picture of white hunters hunting down escaped black slaves out of my head as I responded, "No, no. I've heard this one before. You want me with you to go 'coon' hunting. Nah, not happening, man. You can find me right here. I am not going." They tried to convince me that "coon hunting" was a real thing and the intended target was raccoons, but I had come from an area where Klan stuff was happening. There was no way in the world they were going to get me to do that. I never went with them. I didn't care how much they insisted they were good guys. We just had different cultural perceptions and misperceptions to work through.

In our diversity, we found a common thread, and that was grace. We were born again, and we were all called to do something. There was a purity in that no one was perfect, but we were all striving to be better. In the years when everyone else was partying, we were learning discipline and sacrifice.

I saw God work for me personally at times while at Pillsbury Baptist Bible College. At one point, I was struggling financially. I had a car on campus, which I used to get to work; but the car needed repaired. Midterms were approaching, so it was impractical to take on more hours at work to get extra money. I had not told anyone about my need other than God. One day, I went to my mailbox and found an unmarked envelope with cash inside. No words or explanation came with it. I needed $1,500, and the envelope contained $1,587. If I were to guess, it was probably from an administrator who had been watching me. One might say I was the one kid "born out of season." I didn't have a two-parent family. I did not have a history of generations of family members involved in the ministry as pastors, missionaries, scholars, or apologists. I didn't have a wardrobe full of suits. I did not have what other students were accustomed to having. I valued what they took for granted.

I entered college with a passion for basketball and initially was excited to wear jersey #44, but I lost my love for basketball. The more I learned about God, the less I cared about that ball. Playing ball was about getting acceptance and validation; but when I truly learned about God's love, I found the acceptance and validation I had been searching for. Now, I found myself being more passionate to accept His call to do ministry. I didn't know what that meant or what that would mean for my future, but I surrendered myself to Him.

God had directed me and put it in my heart to go to a Bible college, so I felt very much at home. My mom came up to visit and could not believe it was so cold there. Why would I want to stay there?

The interest in basketball was waning, while the passion for the Bible and ministry was growing. I could not explain it. It was just what was naturally happening.

It didn't bother me being in the all-white environment at college because my high school was pretty much all white. Every school I had been to since elementary school was mostly white, except for the time we spent in Chicago. My town was segregated; but I had always gotten along with people, regardless of skin color. There were blacks who had rejected me saying, "I spoke white," because I spoke with proper, educated English. I basically was too white for some blacks, and I was all too black for some whites. The greatest relationships that I have had throughout the course of my life have had nothing to do with race, but always have had some common connection back to a root of faith. It is a good thing that God does not care about color at all. It was never race. It was always grace! When you understand that we are all made in the image of God, then somehow God must embody all shades and all shades are equal.

ALMOST LEFT COLLEGE

It was 1992 when I went off to college. The NBA had expanded to Minnesota with the 1989 founding of the Timberwolves. A few of the Indiana Pacers' players were traded to start the team. One of the guys I knew at the college knew one of the players. One day, he suggested we go to Minneapolis to a game against the Atlanta Hawks and, perhaps, we could go to an NBA players' party afterwards. I liked the idea. Back then, there was no security team between fans and the players, so you could walk to the end of the bench where the players were.

The team was still rather new, so attendance was low. Christian Laettner was the star for the Minnesota Timberwolves.

One of the players recognized my college friend and said, "Heah, come to the party, man." When we arrived at his house, the player asked my friend, "What's up with your buddy?" Apparently, I must have seemed rather calm in comparison to my friend, who was a little wild. My friend acknowledged, "He's a student with me." Looking back, I am not sure why my fellow college friend was at Bible college. I think he might have been there because he wanted to be a starter on the sports teams, and it was a small school so that was very possible.

He told the basketball player, "I think he is a virgin, and he has never been drunk before." I did not want to seem like a square, so I tried to be convincing, "No, I have done some stuff before."

The basketball player decided to present a challenge to me. He said, "I will give you $4,000 if you can outdrink this little girl over here." I looked at her and estimated that at most she was 4' 11". I decided to double check, "$4,000, cash?" He put the money on the table, "$4,000 cash if you can outdrink her." For clarification, I reconfirmed, "All I have to do is drink more than her." I looked at her, and this seemed like a "slam dunk" (pun intended).

I thought through the scenario before me. I had never had alcohol before, but $4,000 could go a long way. I could do something with that. I even reasoned I could repent with that. He put the money on the table, and they started lining up the drinks. There were twelve or thirteen shot glasses containing liquids of all different colors and a beer at the end. He announced, "The first one to get it done wins."

I had a plan. I would just throw them down, get to the end, win. Well, she was a pro, and I didn't know it. In hindsight, I am confident they knew she was a pro. It was a set up. Size didn't have anything to do with it. She was going so fast, and I was struggling. It was all horrible tasting to me, and it was burning my chest. I was trying so hard because I didn't want to lose the money. I did my best, but she won. Now, I was embarrassed that this little girl won, and I wouldn't get any money. I sat on the couch, contemplating how that could have happened. She was so small. There was no way she should have won.

The NBA players were taking girls back to rooms and leaving some of them with me and the other guys in the main room. I went into this evening completely naïve and was still trying to figure out how I lost the drinking challenge, so I was rather oblivious to what was going on with the women at the party. As I was still there questioning how she drank so much and trying to fathom how a little person could beat me, the room started spinning. I didn't know why I suddenly had a massive headache or why the room was moving around. I was getting dizzy, and closing my eyes did not help. I was sick, and my body wanted to get rid of everything I had consumed.

I was now physically miserable and realized we would have to go back to campus. I was also feeling guilty. I was going to have to tell the president of the college what we had done. I had come to Bible college as a pretty good young man, and I had turned into a sinner. I had never done this stuff before.

The NBA players decided, "We have to get him a girl." This was a bit of a flashback to being with my cousin, but my conscience was already getting to me over the massive consumption of alcohol. The guys picked out a woman and put me in a room with her. She and I started talking. After a little while, one of the guys came back to check on me, and as he prepared to open the door, he called out, "My boy."

As he opened the door, she was accepting Jesus as her Savior. They had their idea of what I was supposed to do with her, but I led her to Jesus. They were done with me, and turning to my college friend, said, "Get him out of here." I was threatening their "fun" by telling the girls about Jesus. "You don't have to do this. God loves you. You do not have to lower yourself to this. You are better that this." The girls realized, "You are right." The guys kicked me out.

I was completely overwhelmed with guilt and believed I wasn't worthy to be a Bible college student. I called Grandma, and she sent me money. I got on a Greyhound bus and headed home. I could not go back to Bible college.

The president of the college called me. When I told him what I had done, he said "Son, you are a new convert, and there are things you do not know. When you mess up, you go to the throne. You do not run home." He told me to come back and so I did.

I am so thankful Dr. Potter did that. Bible college was great for me, not so much for then, but for now. God was at work in everything I was learning, and today I can look at a young Bible college student and be an example for them when they wonder "where can I go in life and what does God have planned for me." With the benefit of hindsight, I can say with confidence, "What God has in store for you is going to cost you. A great calling comes with great challenges, but if you can stand firm, the reward is so worth it."

BRIAN

I left for college two days after high school graduation. I was in such a rush to get to college because I was afraid if I stayed in the area, I would die. Given the community I was in and the conflicts that were happening, I had some kind of premonition that if I stayed, something bad would happen. So many young men who I knew had been murdered because of gang violence, drugs, fights with each other, and a general inability to constructively resolve conflict. I had to get away.

In early March of 1994, I went home on break from Bible college. I was continuing to grow in my faith, and I wanted to invite others to go to church with me while I was in town. I wanted to encourage them and touch their lives. For some reason, one particular person was on my heart. Brian had been a friend of mine from seventh grade through graduation. He had always been friendly. He was a quiet guy, but he was a huge fan of Public Enemy, the rap group.

He looked and dressed just like Chuck D, so that was his nickname. I went by to visit him at his mom's house. He was not there. When he returned, she told him I had stopped by to see him. He came over to my house to see me.

I could tell he was doing well. He had an expensive car and things that represented success for someone just twenty years old; however, those things came at a price. He had become caught up in selling drugs. I shared about Jesus with him and asked him to go to church with me. I wanted to impact him in a positive way. I wanted him to find purpose.

I couldn't shake the huge burden on my heart for him. I insisted, "You have got to come to church with me. You have to promise me. What God has for you is better than this." In the end, I persuaded him to come with me that next morning. Standing there in front of him, I felt compelled to keep talking to him about the Lord. The respect that he had for me and the love we had for each other kept us engaged in conversation. He admired my escape and the fact that I'd found my purpose, something that really fulfilled my life. I was loving the Lord and serving Him. I really felt like I could have led him to Christ right there and then.

There was more in that moment, and I was compelled to keep going, but I decided to put it off for the next day. In my mind, I said, "I will save it for tomorrow. The pastor will be preaching the gospel." I rationalized my plan with I Corinthians 3:6-8, where one planted the seed, another watered it, but it was still God who gave the increase. Today, I was planting.

The next morning, I went to pick him up to take him to church with me. When I got to his home, I could see through the screen door that the main door to the house was open. I could hear screaming inside, but I was not alarmed. There was often chaos around the home because lots of things had happened over the years. He had lost two brothers, who were murdered selling drugs. That morning, though, I didn't know what was going on.

I knocked on the door, and his mom called for me to come in. When I walked in, she was crying, and his younger brothers were visibly upset. I simply asked, "Where is Chuck?" That is when they informed me that someone had killed him the night before. Just hours after he pulled away from my home with the intention of going to church with me the next day, he was gone. I had planned to pick him up because I didn't want to leave anything to chance or have him come up with an excuse at the last minute. However, the ultimate reason he couldn't go to church with me was in front of me. He had come face to face with Heaven's Gates or Hell's Flames.

His death gave me a compelling reason to become very bold about my faith. I felt I had blood on my hands because I waited. The verse immediately came to mind, Ezekiel 3:18, "When I say to a wicked person, 'You will surely die,' and you do not warn them or speak out to dissuade them from their evil ways in order to save their life, that wicked person will die for their sin, and I will hold you accountable for their blood."

I had waited for a sermon to do what a person was assigned to do, and I was the person who had been assigned. I should have continued talking to him and brought him to the point of a decision. I don't know if he continued thinking about our conversation after he left. I don't know if perhaps he made a decision for Christ between our conversation and when he passed. The decision to accept Christ as your personal Lord and Savior can be made anywhere. It does not have to be done within the four walls of a church building or in the presence of a "super spiritual" person. It is between you and God. I hope that one day I get to see him at Heaven's Gates, but for now I do not know.

I might have missed my opportunity with Brian, but I was not going to miss my next opportunity. I preached at his funeral, and I did it in his cadence of speech. Forty-five people came to the Lord.

Brian used to lift weights and was very strong. He was much like a Samson. He caused much more damage to darkness in his death than in his life. His death brought more people into the church, and his death introduced more people to Jesus.

RAZOR'S EDGE

M y passion for evangelism opened a door to something I never would have imagined.

Harvest Productions, a film ministry of Evangelical Baptist Missions, "was founded in 1975 by Don Ross to produce high-quality Christian videos for use as ministry tools." (https://hpmvideos.com/about/) All of the organization's work is completed by volunteers. Those who look like employees are effectively missionaries raising their own support. The film crews work on very much the same model.

A small film crew with a passion for evangelism reached out to various Bibles colleges looking for college-aged black people to cast in various roles for Razor's Edge, a short movie about the true-life testimony of a black barber who was very violent in his youth and became a Christian. During the filming, I had the opportunity to meet the actual man whose testimony we were re-enacting.

I had always been into sports, so getting a small part in a movie was a whole new thing. I was cast to play a coworker and partying friend of the main character. It was interesting to be given a speaking part where I, a Bible college student, was part of his "serious sin" crowd and mocked the Christian coworker, "a holy roller," "who was quiet as a mouse and straight as an arrow."

Being part of the cast opened my eyes to a new world. It was there that I met other people my age from other Bible colleges. Until that time, I didn't even know there were other black students in Bible colleges. I was one of only two black students at Pillsbury Baptist; but, while working on the movie, I met some black students from Bob Jones University. I was very impressed with how polished and professional they were.

When the movie came out, I was very excited and was once again inviting people to church and filling another school bus, just as I had done as a teenager. It was so personally rewarding to see so many people coming to Christ.

https://www.youtube.com/watch?v=XE0MOxPAkw0

TRANSFERRING TO BOB JONES

Pillsbury Baptist Bible College was a small Bible college, and it was starting to suffer financially. At the same time, I was sensing a need to move to another place to continue to grow. They were phenomenal in their willingness to accept me, a young high school graduate who was still very new to his faith and needed discipling. It had been the perfect place for me to learn, grow, and mature. While there, I developed a greater understanding of scripture, a greater command of it, and the ability to deliver it; but now I was ready for a larger school.

Through working on the Razor's Edge, I met Bob Jones University students. My pastor at the time had become a huge advocate for Bob Jones University and really pushed for me to go. He said, "I think you would be phenomenal there. I think they would benefit from you." My pastor even introduced me to Dr. Bob shortly before Dr. Bob passed.

Bob Jones University was much more polished. I would not have been accepted right out of high school. I would have needed a greater education, more Biblical knowledge, more background in my faith, a better understanding of customs and dress code, and the list goes on. Pillsbury was the steppingstone for me to advance in those areas, which made acceptance at Bob Jones possible. I visited the campus and knew this was the next step for me. They gave me a scholarship, which made it possible for me to attend. There were strict rules, but that was fine with me. I was laser focused on why I was going to school. I knew I wanted to do ministry.

Bob Jones University was so devout. It gave me discipline and structure. We woke up early and had white-glove inspections of our rooms. Studying was finished by 9 p.m., and it was considered cheating if you studied after 9 p.m. Bedtimes were early so you could be up early the next morning.

Each night, we had devotions in our rooms with our roommates. One guy would be the prayer captain and lead the time of prayer, while another would lead the devotions. We would then go into the hall and continue the fellowship.

We did not have televisions, so it was easy to get into "the bubble," as we said. We were focused on our education, studying, and ministry. I didn't know anything about what was happening in popular culture and music. For someone who had always stayed current on professional basketball, it was strange to not know what was going on in the sports world. I can remember hearing that Michael Jordan had returned to basketball, but we never saw it. We were focused on our reason for being at the university.

This was the perfect setting for me. It was like a boot camp where you study the Bible, are challenged, are held accountable in public and in private, which results in you improving as a person and believer to equip you for your calling. I was not looking for social connections and things like that. I was there for a purpose, and I was going to stay focused.

I became so serious about ministry and memorization of scriptures that, at one point, my uncle Robert came to visit me on campus because he was concerned that I had joined a cult. Gradually, my family realized, "No, it is not a cult. James is just completely sold out on Jesus and learning."

Bob Jones University was strict when it came to listening to music. Most of the groups that I had grown up listening to were basically banned. Culturally, that was a real challenge for me. The things that I had grown up with as commonplace, they considered to be sinful. The black gospel music I grew up listening to was not allowed. There was a provision for a student to bring in music and let the music department decide whether they could have it on campus. It was strict, and I opted to learn about the music genres that were already approved.

One of the other actors in the Razor's Edge worked at the radio station on campus and helped me get a job there. I was assigned to the opera hour. I didn't know the first thing about opera, but my job was to get on and talk about "what pathos" in her voice. I had no idea what that was and just read the script with whatever was written. I would also read the weather report or whatever else they had for me. That might have been the first clue that my voice was unique, but I still had not caught on to it. As I look back, God was leading me along with crumbs of opportunity to point me toward His direction for my life. I just didn't lean fully in to see what He was doing.

Partially because of my radio job and partially because it was an available activity on campus, I found myself falling in love with opera. Even if I didn't know what they were saying, I would go to the operas on campus. I went from thinking "What is this?" to "What great pathos!" or, in more regular English, "What great ability to evoke emotion in the audience!" The university supported the classical arts, and while I could have focused on things that could be construed as negative because it was so different than what I grew up with, for me, it was really unique, and I embraced it.

I loved the discipline. I loved the structure. I loved the sports and activities we had on campus.

It was interesting that 25 years after graduating from Bob Jones University, I happened to be in Worcester, Massachusetts for the grand opening of a new prosthetic office and encountered a van full of Bob Jones University students. We happened to be staying in the same hotel, and it was a joy to have breakfast with them. I reminisced about the "good old days" and learned how many things have changed. I learned that guys are permitted to wear jeans on campus. For me, that was a "Wait! You mean Bob Jones let up on the rules?" It felt like they had backslidden. When I was a student, I wore a suit and tie every day. There was not a time that I wasn't professionally dressed. To see the current students dressed like normal young people was shocking, but it was also great to see that the things they released were preferences and style that are not specifically addressed in the Bible, anyway.

When I was there, I never went to the movies or even thought about it. Not everything was forbidden, but not everything would add value to preparing you for the mission field. Your mission field might be in what is traditionally thought of as the mission field, like overseas ministry, street ministry, or pastoring a church, but your mission field might also be the business world or settings where you would be around affluent people with Ivy League backgrounds. I was being prepared to relate to people from all walks of life in all types of settings.

Bob Jones University taught me to look critically at the sermons of great preachers, to study content and accuracy. I learned not to be swayed by their popularity or public persona. Sometimes, men I had previously held in high regard were brought down a level as I studied the content of their messages and their theology. Everything must be rooted in the actual scriptures and the accurate interpretation thereof.

Bob Jones was an eye-opening experience for me, and I learned self-sufficiency. I roomed with some guys who were really committed to ministry and what they wanted to do with their lives. I did have one interesting roommate who enlisted in the Marines while attending Bob Jones University. He had decided that he wasn't going to let the military bootcamp affect him, saying, "No matter what, they are not going to be able to change me. They are not going to brainwash me."

We saw a very different reality. By the time they finished shaving his head and he returned, he was a different person. I remember he would come with us to church and on the way back he would say, "Stop the car. This Marine wants to run." He would get out of the car, in a suit, and take off running the three miles back to campus. It could be raining, and he was in a suit with slick shoes, but that did not seem to matter to him anymore. I would say, "Man, it is raining." He would defiantly respond, "It does not rain on a

Marine." We would get into arguments, and he would bark back, "I don't feel the rain." In complete futility, I tried to remind him, "You said you would not be brainwashed. What happened to that guy? Now you are out here talking stupid. Do you actually think there is no rain on you?" He would reiterate, "Not on a Marine." All I could respond with was "Yeah, okay."

A part of me desired that same mental toughness. I had always wished I could serve in the military, but being an amputee meant I was not permitted to enlist. On some level, his irrationality about the rain was not unlike my arguments with mom over Hulk Hogan.

There was one good thing my Marine friend had going for him. He had developed good physical fitness habits. As believers, we should take care of our bodies, which are a temple for the Holy Spirit. Our body is not ours. It is on loan. We need to be a good steward of it so we can be a good soldier. A soldier goes to war, and everywhere we go is a battlefield. The battlefield is for someone's destiny.

Romantic relationships proved interesting at Bob Jones. At that time, interracial dating was not really allowed. If you wanted to date someone outside of your race, you had to get parental permission from both families, and there was a lot involved with that. No one I knew tried it or even entertained the thought. Women lived on one side of campus, and men lived on the other. If you wanted to go on a date, you had to take a chaperone. There was a dating parlor where you could meet girls. It was a collection of couches, that the school provided, where you could sit and talk to a young lady, while chaperones walked around, keeping a close watch. Their watch was close, but nothing else was. While in the dating parlor, you had to abide by a six-inch rule. You could not be any closer than six inches to her.

There was one black girl who came on campus; but there were six black males, a total of eight if you included those from Africa. At first, all of us guys thought she was not very attractive, but as time went on and with her being the only option for us, things changed. There were formal events that students could attend with a young lady, and since she was the only one for us, the competition got fierce. I can remember saying to some of the guys, "Remember, we said she is not attractive," but then I started noticing guys were meeting up with her, walking with her, carrying her bookbag, etc. It became a competition. If there was only going to be one possible wife available on campus, there could only be one winner.

We all went after this girl. She went from getting no attention to a full blitz from all the black males. She requested that we all write out our testimony and a five-year plan for our lives upon graduation. She had us putting together our resumes and vison boards, not to marry her, but just to have the opportunity to go on a date with her.

Eventually, this competition caused us to start turning on each other. We were all good friends, but as events would come up where we could take a date, things would change. We started saying things to her like, "I have not seen Jermaine reading his Bible as much as he should. Just saying. Maybe that is not a big deal to you, but if you want a husband who loves the Lord, I am sure you do not want Jermaine." Another might say, "James does not get good grades." It got bad. We were not exemplifying the Christian character we were studying at school to master. When she decided who she wanted to date, the rest of us knew we couldn't be friends with him anymore and, thus, we went on our way. We competed for that one girl, and then, when we lost her, that was it.

I received my first Klan letter while at Bob Jones. A Klan member wrote and threatened to do something to me. I don't remember the details, but the basic idea was I would be shot, killed, or whatever if I did not go away. I thought it was interesting, but I wasn't scared. My attitude was, "Yeah, right, whatever." I really did blow it off. It was going to take more than that to scare me off.

Being very confident in my identity, I heard that there was a church nearby the campus that people said was not very welcoming to black people, so I decided to go to that church. This church was rumored to always have an outdoor section for black people. I guess that had been the case at some point, but I went inside. I sat in the front row, kind of in defiance, but, also, I had read stories about how Billy Graham had torn down the lines of segregation in the South, so I saw no reason not to join everyone else inside the church. In 1952, Billy Graham took a dramatic stand at a crusade in Jackson, Mississippi, when he physically removed the rope meant to separate the blacks and whites at the crusade. (https://billygrahamlibrary.org/billy-graham-racism/) It was rumored that some people didn't care for him because of actions like that; however, he played an integral role in reconciling people of faith and removing that aspect of bigotry.

Armed with that head knowledge, I decided "Yeah. I am going to this church, and I'm sitting in the front row." So, I did. I heard something from people along the lines of "Do not do that again. Respect their customs or their beliefs," but I didn't care. I was unafraid, and I was fervent about my faith. I was not going to be defined or limited by my race. I only know one thing, and that is grace. Grace does not discriminate. I was adamant that I was going to sit in that front row. I was going to be the first black person to do it. And there was not a person who was going to do anything to me for doing it.

POST-COLLEGE PLAN

Upon graduation from college, I thought, I will marry. We will do ministry and serve in the inner city. We will start a church from the ground up. I learned, though, that sometimes life does not go the way we plan.

I needed a job and was hired at a Christian school in Indianapolis to be their physical education teacher and teach an academic class. After a season there, an opportunity opened to become a Christian school administrator in Syracuse, New York.

I was contacted by the senior pastor of a church in Syracuse. He was excited by my educational background and my experience working in a Christian school. His vision for the church included building a school, and he saw me as the perfect person to fill the role of assistant pastor. He suggested I move to Syracuse. Everything was set. Unbeknownst to me, that was not the full truth.

I loaded up my U-Haul and headed from Indiana to New York.

When I arrived, I walked into the church, where they were in the process of voting on the two candidates for assistant pastor. I was the senior pastor's pick; however, there was another candidate who was local and had a good following. While both of us could preach, the other gentleman had musical gifts and could also fill the role of music minister. Given our ability to preach, both of us were duplicate talent to the senior pastor; however, the other gentleman's musical ability was a strong selling point for the others in church leadership. My school experience really only fit with the senior pastor's vision, and the rest of the church leadership was not yet in agreement with that vision. While they were inside voting, I found myself standing in the parking lot with a U-Haul containing all my worldly possessions, six hundred miles and nine hours from home, wondering if I actually had a job.

The senior pastor decided to play on emotions and leverage a sense of obligation in those voting and called me inside. He went on to explain, "The kid has already moved here." This was my entre into church politics, something I strongly dislike to this day.

I was so conditioned out of Bible college that the senior pastor is supposed to be respected, revered, and honored. The actions I was seeing play out in front of me felt in stark contrast to what I had learned to be the proper character of someone in that role. I witnessed him take things said in confidence in counseling sessions and put them into his Sunday sermons. While not naming the person, he may include enough context clues and descriptions to allow the average person in the church to clearly identify the person and situation being referenced. As someone so new out of Bible college with a head knowledge of the ideal and being exposed to something that did not feel even close to the ideal, I wrestled internally.

There were only about 75 people attending the church at the time, but there was enough money to cover having both a senior pastor and an assistant. I remember one Sunday the offerings happened to be down and the senior pastor came to me and told me that he would not be able to pay me that week. "Sorry, Brother, maybe next week." It became a regular yoyo of "This Sunday looks like we will be able to pay you ... Not this Sunday, sorry again."

Even though they were not paying me, the pastor still wanted me to assume the full-time responsibilities of the church. It was not easy to support a family on consistent work with inconsistent pay. I would hear the cliché, "You gotta trust the Lord." I was fasting, but it was not by choice, so I started looking for another job to supplement the income from the church. I was willing to take on a part-time job for a season because as I saw it, once the church grew, they would be able to consistently pay me and make good on the past-due compensation.

One day, the pastor had a stroke, and he would obviously be unable to handle his regular duties for a season. His wife worked there also and handled various secretarial and administrative duties. She had her own medical issues to tend to and now was pulled away to support him in his recovery. I began to cover all the roles. I was "gung-ho." Whatever we need to do, I would get it done.

While he was recovering, I began to preach. Immediately, our church attendance grew. We went from 75 to 330 over the next several weeks. The offerings increased substantially. The senior pastor was still struggling with his speech, so he would write. At the same time, he took advantage of the growth and improved financial position of the church to have the deacons recommend a raise for him and his wife.

It became obvious that the senior pastor was concerned about his future and, in his insecurity, started booking other people to fill in for Sunday preaching. He said to me, "Brother Dixon, you will be preaching on the fourth Sunday." When the congregation figured out the pattern, some would only come on the fourth Sunday. Finally, one day he approached me and said, "Brother, God has called me here, and He does not want the vision spread amongst brethren. He has called me here to shepherd, and it would be best if you go and not tell anyone that you left."

He referred me to put in my resume at another church. "Go there," he said, "but do not tell anyone where you have gone." He was concerned that some of the new attendees of the church had become loyal to me and not to the church itself; and if I mentioned where I went, they would follow me. He hoped to have the new people absorbed into the crowd as his church members.

My Bible college training taught me to never question authority; and, thus, I agreed to his wishes. When I left, I was confused. I didn't understand how this had occurred, and I was struggling to adjust. Even though that church had paid me haphazardly, it did help toward the bottom line of supporting myself and my family. Now, suddenly, that income was instantaneously gone.

I learned later that he characterized my disappearance as "demons having forsaken the things of God to shipwreck the ministry." He suggested that I did not love the things of the Lord. It really bothered me that he characterized my disappearance as abandonment of ministry when, in reality, it was his hand pushing me out.

I candidated for a new church. Candidating is when you submit your resume, and then might be asked to come preach. They will then decide whether they believe you are the right person to lead their congregation. There were two candidates who were being considered for the position. The other gentleman was a man in his fifties, who had been a janitor in the school system. Unfortunately, he never had the opportunity to learn to read. He was well known in the community, and his extended family was influential in that church, and they wanted him to be the pastor. I was something of an outsider and only 26 years old. My resume included the fact that I had gone to Bible college. Some would look on that favorably as taking the initiative to develop my God-given gift, but there is another perspective that says, "He went to school to learn to preach. If God called him, he would not need to go to school." All the things that would make you a strong candidate in the logical, intellectual world seemed to be working against me in this setting. I heard the comments, "He may be book called, but my cousin is God called."

The leadership of the church scheduled a picnic where the candidates were invited to come, interact with, and talk to all of the families. I figured I was there to interact with everyone, so I started meeting people. I met some of the children and was shaking their hands when the people who wanted to vote for me pulled me aside. They told me to get away from the children because people might think I am just a youth pastor. I was new to this candidating thing, so I made mental notes for myself, "Okay. Do not shake hands with children, not the children."

I was further advised to go befriend "that guy over there" because he was really influential. This felt like politicking, which is not my style, so I decided I wasn't going to do it. I was going to be me, nothing more and nothing less. I was going to engage and interact with everybody. I was even going to go say hello to the gentleman candidating against me. My gestures and kind words were rebuffed. He was sizing me up, would not shake my hand, ignored me, and walked off. This was shocking to me and did not seem like good behavior for a future pastor. I thought for sure that would be the nail in the coffin for him.

The Sunday when I was scheduled to preach came, and I preached an expository message that was from the soul. Since it was a black congregation, I spoke about the need for men. We need men who will stand for God, men who will return to the community of the congregation, and men who will then move out into the community to reach others. We need solid men at the core of the church, which becomes something you can build from. The bottom line, we need men.

I took the themes that were popular at the time and adapted them, altering "Uncle Sam wants you" to be "Jesus wants you." He does not just want you to attend with your wife at Easter, or if we are playing basketball or watching the Superbowl together. Jesus wants you. He needs a few good men. While I was using the popular phrases, it was from the heart, and it was connecting with the guys. My scripture text was centered around Isaiah 6:8 "Then I heard the voice of the Lord saying, "Whom shall I send? And who will go for us?" And I said, "Here am I. Send me!" I reiterated how God just needs a few good men and our prayer should be, "God use me. I can change things. I can break generational curses." My sermon was organized with an open, middle, and close. It had conviction, charisma, emotion, and passion. I gave an invitation, and 36 men stood up to accept Christ.

I was so encouraged by the response of the people when one of the ladies yelled out, "If you whoop, you got the church." But I was not a whooper, and I was not going to do it. I preach God and His word. That is it. I don't need to rely on a stereotypical style of speaking or rhythmical cadence to get everyone excited and emotional at church, as if that is somehow more spiritual. If you want me, this is it. I preach the word of God. I will preach the Biblical concepts. I will preach the truth because it is what it is. God says it. That is it. No whooping necessary.

The following Sunday the other gentleman preached. I stopped in to hear him. It was the same crowd of people. He started in whopping style with, "Humpty Dumpty sat on a wall. Humpty Dumpty had a great fall. Humpty Dumpty found out he was nothing without Jesus at all. Come on somebody..." He continued like that for about fifteen minutes, and then started screaming and dancing. They voted him in. The next Sunday, his first as the senior pastor, he preached the same message. The next Sunday, the same message. The fourth Sunday, they called me and said, "What do you think about starting the process again with you versus another?" I said, "No, you guys chose a guy who could not read or write. How is he going to preach the word of God if he does not know what it says?"

Realizing I had a point they informed me, "Yeah, we..., but we cannot just vote you in." I reminded them that they had two finalists and one of them had obviously just disqualified himself, so how many do you have? They continued with, "Yeah ... but ... our church ... the way it works... They want to find another candidate to go up against you." I pulled myself from candidacy. "No, I am not doing this." I said, "I will start my own church."

During this season of working in schools and churches, I

unfortunately learned the hard way that these positions, while great for kingdom impact, did not pay well. To supplement my income, I took a sales job on the side. I quickly realized that I could make more money in a few months in commissions working part time than I could make annually teaching or preaching. Over time and over the challenges of the church jobs, I reversed my perspective around working and volunteering. While I started off being paid for ministry and doing other things part time, I shifted to working in sales full time and volunteering for ministry part time.

I discovered that my charisma and skills of persuasion would be handsomely rewarded in the commercial world; however, I struggled internally. I was making considerable income in sales; however, I felt like I was cheapening my evangelistic skills as I talked business leaders into five-year contracts for long distance phone service. Getting the second job and getting commissions created a great pathway for me, but it also left me feeling empty.

MARRIAGE

Coming out of Bible college, I was ready for the next phase of life. I had been conditioned that the next thing I needed was a wife with whom I could do ministry. Up to this point, I had always struggled with relationships because it always felt like my leg was a barrier to being fully accepted. If anyone liked me, I would just accept it. I didn't feel confident pursuing relationships because I was sure that somehow I would eventually be rejected.

My first wife was considerably older and already had children from a prior relationship. Within two years, we met, dated, became engaged, and married. I didn't have a great example of marriage in my early years and didn't really know how to know if this was the right person for me. I leaned heavily on the advice and judgment of some of the older men of my church.

This is where I learned the danger of church. The local church and Christ are separate. A brick-and-mortar church is a building, and that is not what Christ died for. Ideally, the leadership of the local church is following Christ, but just because someone has the title of reverend or pastor, that doesn't guarantee he or she knows what Christ has for you. While I can get counsel from the men around me, my ultimate source of counsel and direction must be Christ.

I was definitely in over my head with the marriage. In hindsight, I realized there were people playing matchmaker who I felt I could trust, but I am not so sure they really had the best interest of either one of us at heart. I did the best I knew to be a husband. To fill in the gaps, I sought out great teaching material.

DAUGHTER ARRIVES

As the day of official fatherhood approached, I couldn't help but be concerned for my child's limbs.

I was so devalued as a person, so unaccepted, so rejected, so alone in my development from childhood through to my adult life. Even though I had gotten up and preached and shared my testimony of salvation, I always felt like I still was not fully accepted. I had struggled so much, feeling rejected for being an amputee, and I didn't want that for my child. I wanted my child to have legs and be able to walk like everyone else.

I couldn't contain my joy when I saw that my daughter was born with fully functioning legs. When I left the hospital late that night, I was so happy that I ran out into the middle of the streets of Syracuse, New York and danced. The Bible talks about how David danced before the Lord. I danced because my God gave me my baby and my baby's got legs. My baby would not have to go through what I went through.

I had decided when I was eight that if I ever had a daughter, she would be named after my grandmother and, thus, my baby girl was named Kiziah. Elizabeth would be her middle name after John the Baptist's mother. My daughter's name reflects the truth: I am beautiful, and God is my light.

Seeing my baby with legs brought much-needed healing into my heart. As much as I tried to ignore it and not talk about it, there was always a piece of me that was not whole. The same God who saved me was also making me whole that night without my realizing it. I could suddenly identify with the men as they stood at the tomb of Jesus and asked, "Sir, we perceive that you are a gardener," not realizing they were talking to Jesus. Jesus had been speaking to my heart all along, and I hadn't realized it was Him. I had been willing to settle for the dead body of Jesus being raised and me just being a Christian, not realizing that there was a mission so much greater that He was preparing me to pursue.

Many years later, I was again faced with concern for the limbs of my children. While my son, James, was born underweight, I was just as excited as I was with Kiziah to see that he had all his limbs. Then God blessed me with Jeremiah, my favorite biblical character's name, and he, too, was born with all of his limbs. My tribe was complete, and my heart gained a forever smile.

BROOKLYN TAB

Unfortunately, marriage and the birth of my daughter did not lead to living "happily ever after." Things began to fall apart; and, before long, the marriage crumbled, and I was separated from my daughter. All my dreams for great fulfillment in ministry had been crushed with politics and human egos getting in the way of God's design. I was questioning my faith and in a challenging season of struggling.

I found my way to the back row of a moderately-sized church in upstate New York that was packed with people wanting to hear the Brooklyn Tabernacle Choir. I was just one of a few hundred in the building. The lead singer that night was Calvin Hunt, and he shared his testimony of being on drugs and what God had done in his life.

As the concert was nearing the end, I got up to leave. Suddenly, Calvin Hunt pointed to me and said, "You, please stay." I was caught off guard and thought he was just correcting me for bad manners. It occurred to me that perhaps a collection plate was going to be passed, and it would be rude of me to leave so abruptly. Shortly thereafter, I realized he wanted me to stay because he wanted to say something to me specifically. He came down off the stage and walked over to me. He said, "I have never done this in my life. I do not know who you are, but as I was singing, God said 'there is something big in you, but whatever it is that you are called to do, you are going to go through it in order to become it.' That is all I know. God has never spoken to me about a particular person before, but that is what I must tell you."

Here it goes, I thought. *This is another one of those guys probably saying something all the time because if he knew what I was going through...* Having Calvin Hunt tell me I was going to be something big felt like false doctrine. After all, how could I be something big in life when I felt so small?

I had just lost a custody battle because of my naivety. I had trusted that a lawyer was working on my behalf, but instead he used my naivety against me. I was feeling so betrayed. Even more, I felt like I could not be used by God. I had failed in the covenant of marriage, and if I could not be a husband, how could I be a minister? How could I serve? What do I do with my life now?

In my pain and hopelessness, I developed a plan. I was going to go live my life and do whatever. I was not being accepted by people. In my mind, I could not be loved because my leg kept that from happening. Everything in my life had just fallen into failure. My Bible college training and preparation were for nothing. I had been telling myself all this time that I had helped others, but maybe it was all little more than a Band-Aid over my own wounds. I was so low that I didn't feel like I could make it.

I turned my back on God because I felt like God had turned His back on me. I found myself in relationships I never should have entered and saw a side of my character that I did not like. I was following a trail of sin crumbs that was leading me down a path of destruction, and I was leaving destruction behind me. As the years went by, I felt like I couldn't go back or find my way back even if I wanted to. At times, I would try to do the right things or want to do the right things, but everything seemed like a struggle.

There were times I would be out late at night, and, inevitably at midnight, the gospel hour would come on the radio. The DJ might start talking about how Jesus was right there with me in the room and conviction would overtake me.

Interestingly, God kept trying to pull me back. Every time I tried to go to a club or a bar or places where people were, somebody would inevitably say, "This is not for you," or "You do not belong here." I could not seem to get myself into certain trouble, no matter how hard I tried. There were people who would not smoke or drink around me, but here I was trying to fit in and be like everybody else. No matter how many times I tried to explain "I am just like you guys," they didn't seem to buy it. There was something about me that they saw that I could not see in myself.

Suddenly, I got word that my grandmother was not doing well.

GRANDMA

While I was out doing my thing, living in New York, my grandmother called me and asked, "Do you remember the promise?" There was only one promise I had ever given my grandmother and that was when I was eight years old. The same day I told her if I ever had a daughter, I would name her after her, I also told her I would never let anyone put her in a nursing home. It was the one thing I had promised her, and now Grandma was afraid it was going to happen. My mom and uncles would have never done that, but Grandma was afraid. There was talk of putting her in rehab, and rehab often took place in nursing homes. She was overwhelmed with fears of being abandoned. While it was not going to be her reality, I was so close to her that when she got scared, it made me come home to make sure Grandma was okay.

I transferred my job from New York to Indiana. I was doing well financially, but I was doing horrible spiritually. I was top in sales, but I was bankrupt in my soul. As I watched Grandma struggle, I knew I needed to pray. I needed to be able to talk to God about it because I didn't want to lose her. I had lost all confidence in my own relationship with God and felt so distant from Him, so I called a church to ask them to pray for her.

I then decided to try to bargain with God. "God, I will go back to church, but I need you to do me a favor. Please heal Grandma." I even made Him an offer that He could take years off my life if He would give them to her. I just couldn't imagine life without her and didn't want Him to take her away from me.

I started praying, and I started believing, even though it really didn't seem like Grandma was doing so well. Gradually, she started improving, and there was talk from the nurses that she would end up going home. Then, suddenly, she took another bad turn.

One day, I walked into the room and found her sitting there, motioning to me. I couldn't tell what she was saying because she had a trach in then. I couldn't make out the words she was trying to say, but I felt like her motions were indicating that she wanted me to pull the plug. She had had enough. She was discouraged and down. I said, "Grandma I cannot do that."

I had never seen Grandma down. That was not her. I didn't want her to give up, although on some level, I understood wanting to give up because I had been there myself. She had always been the one pulling me through, so, I was not going to let her give up. Fortunately, that moment passed.

With things looking up, I could be grateful. "God, Thank you, Man. You are working. Grandma is doing better. Thank you." Unfortunately, in that season, how I felt about God at any given moment was tied to my personal circumstances and emotions in the moment and not to who He is and the price He paid for me.

I had been spending a lot of my time at the hospital. My mom realized I needed a break and suggested I get out of there and go do something, perhaps go out on a date.

Back then, we had pagers, not cell phones. Mom said, "If something is wrong, we will page you. If we send you a message that is all 1s, that means get here quickly because bad things are happening."

That seemed like a good plan, and I really did need a break. I left and drove to a movie theater about 35 minutes away. I remember buying popcorn and sitting down. Perhaps another 15 minutes passed, and the distraction the movie gave me was interrupted by the pager.

When I saw that it was all 1s, I got in the car and started driving back to the hospital as fast as I could. Normally, it would be a 35-minute drive, but not that night.

After I walked into the main entrance of the hospital, I found the whole family gathered in the family lounge, embracing each other and crying. My immediate reaction was "No. This is not happening. I cannot accept it. I have to see it." As I walked into her room, the funeral director was zipping the body bag. The very hospital that welcomed me into the world was ushering my grandmother out.

One of my aunts turned to me and said, "If you had been here…" She had believed that my prayers and presence had much more power and my being gone had taken Grandma away from us all. Everyone was embracing each other, but no one noticed that I was not being touched. I was the minister of the family and was expected to be strong for them. I was supposed to know what to do, but at this moment, I did not. I was merely in my late twenties, and this weight was too much for me.

My aunt's words echoed through my mind. People were starting to fight, and relationships were crumbling around me. Grandma was no longer the glue to hold everyone together. Outside of Mom, where would I go now for unconditional love? Grandma had always given me unconditional love and acceptance. While growing up, I had spent so much time with her, learning from her and talking to her. All that was gone, and everyone was fighting over stuff. This upset me because I knew her legacy was her faith and her example, not her stuff.

I spoke at Grandma's funeral. The place was packed. The only way I was able to make it through was to look at faraway faces. There was a sense of duty, but there was also anger. "God, I only asked you for one thing, and You did not give it."

That's when I made the decision to walk away from ministry. I was angry at God and done with Him; however, He was not done with me. He has a way of calling you back by showing you that He has already done more than enough. He shows you He is still with you. My grandmother's suffering was finished, and her body was gone, but her legacy was not. It would just take more time for me to once again find my way back to live out the very things she had instilled in me.

FINDING MY WAY BACK TO FAITH

Grandma went to Heaven in 2000, and the next two years of my life were self-destructive as I struggled with grief and being angry at God for taking her. I needed to find a church to ease my sense of guilt for not living up to what I knew I was called to do, but I wanted to hide in the anonymity of a large church. I wanted to be there, but I wanted to be hidden. I felt like a megachurch would allow me to be present but not be seen.

I found my megachurch, where even a Sunday school class might have 60 to 70 people. It would be easy to hide in a group that size. Unfortunately, the classes were being led by volunteers, many of whom had wonderful hearts but very poor training. I couldn't escape the fact that my Bible training was now part of my DNA, and I could not sit idly by and allow incorrect theology to be given to those who were there to learn and grow. The teacher would say things, and I would raise my hand and inevitably begin with, "It is not quite like that."

One Sunday while sitting in the class, a woman started interpreting the verse in 1 Kings 18:42, where Elijah is praying for rain to come and end the drought. In the New International Version, the text says, "Elijah climbed to the top of Carmel, bent down to the ground and put his face between his knees." This well-meaning woman went on to explain that Elijah was taking the birthing position of a woman. The Bible college student in me could not be quiet. "Yeah. No. That is eisegesis." Everyone looked at me as if to say, what is that? "Exegeting a text is where you read what is in the scripture considering the original context to determine the meaning or intent, while eisegesis is where you just make up whatever you want, putting your own ideas into the text." I was confident there was never going to be a point where God would have a man pretend to give birth to a baby. As far I was concerned, her interpretation was not just wrong, it was evil.

I explained what the text says. He prayed in humility, realizing, God, I need you. It was the same humility Samson needed to get a prayer through, "Lord, remember me." It is the feeling of distance and absence between you and God and then asking God to do something for His name's sake or for His glory and not yours. God can respond to those types of prayers, even when you have been wayward. Elijah was not praying to benefit himself. It was for everyone else. They desperately needed rain because their water sources had dried up. God saw Elijah's humility and selfless heart and answered his prayer.

The other students in the class were hungry for more knowledge and understanding of the scriptures, so every Sunday I would be asked to recap or say something. Within a matter of weeks, the class was turned over to me, and it went from sixty to seventy adults in the class to two to three hundred. One day, the senior pastor approached me and said, "I have been hearing about you, and we have a Bible institute. I would like you to teach on the Old Testament."

I had been so frustrated with God over not answering my one prayer to heal my grandmother. I had been so wayward. I had gone through my own version of hell and become the subject of accusations, lies, and character attacks. Now, here I was being asked to step back into a ministry role yet again.

I truly understood being the prodigal son. I was feeling the call of God to come back into relationship with Him, but I was also feeling guilt. The more time I was in that environment of the Sunday school classroom answering questions or giving my thoughts, the more I felt myself wanting to study so I could give concrete Bible-based reasons, rather than just my opinion. If I could point to specific scripture, there would be no argument because everyone in the room had already accepted the idea that the Bible was God's infallible word. Pointing to what the text says is not an opinion. God does not need our feelings to agree with His word. We just have to accept His word.

As this prodigal son returned, doors to serve began opening. It was not long before the senior pastor of this 15,000-member church asked me to sit in the pulpit with him. This was a big moment for me. I never envisioned doing that, even in my days in Bible college. After my prodigal season, I definitely did not think I would be back doing ministry.

I was brought onto the research team and started working on material for the senior pastor. I would write messages, sermons, and illustrations that they used. I was studying more and forcing myself to grow. As I was doing that, I started to get over the ill feelings I had toward God. I realized I had made an unreasonable demand of Him when I said to Him, "Heal her!" I had an argument I had felt was reasonable. "It's me asking for this God, not someone else. This is me. I went to Bible college when You sent me. I followed the path. I did these things for You. I did my best. Yes, I messed up some, but still I asked that of You, and You could have given that to me." I realized that my heart had been selfish. Everything was about me and not what was best for my grandmother or what God's will was for her life. God did not owe me my grandmother. I owed Him me.

I realized I did not know how to deal with the grief of losing my grandmother. I was expected to be strong for everyone else, but there was no one I could turn to during that grief, so I went wayward. I didn't yet understand that even pastors need pastors to help them through tough times. Without a support system for myself and men to whom I could be accountable, I found myself operating in sin and doing things that I never would have done. Now that I had found my way back, I could not study without repentance. The more I studied, the more I knew I was wrong. The more I opened the Bible so I could prepare for others, the more I was being changed. That accountability of having to be prepared for someone else became a great thing for me—though I did not think so at the time.

REVIVAL

I was so actively involved with the megachurch ministry that I was now somewhat recognizable. One day, a pastor of a small church in Muncy, Indiana who looked up to the megachurch showed up at our Bible institute. He knew that I was involved with the leadership team because he had seen me in the pulpit. He was going to be holding revival services and knew that getting our senior pastor would be almost impossible. His small church could not afford the speaking fee of our senior pastor. He approached me and said, "I would love it if you could come speak one night at our church. We are having a revival." It was a small church, and I casually said, "Yeah, I will do it."

I invited my mom and stepdad to come with me to the small church. There was a really small crowd, but it was a sincere group, hungry for revival. My message was about repentance. I was talking about my own path. I remember saying, "If there was ever a time in your life that you were closer to God than you are right now, then you are backslidden, and the reason I know is because I have lived backslidden." As simple as that message might have been, there was a tremendous response from the people.

At the conclusion of my sermon, the pastor asked, "Can you do one more night? Just one more night. God is using you here." The next evening, there was standing room only in the church. People who had attended the first night brought more people. It was another great service, and the pastor asked me to come back for a third night.

On the third night, there were so many people that they had to move me to a different area so they could make room for everyone. The church sanctuary was full. The fellowship hall was full. They were running closed circuit TV to every other place they could put people in the building; meanwhile, I was preaching from the kitchen that was attached to the fellowship hall, and I was preaching my heart out.

I had patterned my message after Jonathan Edwards, the great American revivalist preacher of the early 1700s. I wrote a more modern version of his famous "Sinners in the hands of an angry God." My take on it was that God is angry because we refuse to repent. We may feel justified, but "Does thou well to be angry with God?" I was still preaching to myself. Was I really doing well being angry in my own Jonah-like rebellion? I wanted revenge for what had been done to me. I wanted Him to do things my way and answer this prayer request and that prayer request, all for selfish reasons. I questioned His wisdom, but still God is God. If He had answered my prayer to bring back my grandmother, it would have been miserable for her. She would have had to leave Heaven and the presence of God to suffer death again, not unlike Lazarus.

Preaching in that small country church opened more doors, and my ministry and speaking opportunities increased. The pastor of the small church often put videos from his services on local public broadcasting for free. "It just so happened" that a gentleman who was a member of, at the time, the largest African American church in America, was passing through the area and happened to flip channels when a video of me preaching was airing. He heard me, looked me up, and reached out to me.

He was what we would call in church circles the senior pastor's armor bearer. He was a right-hand man to the senior pastor. That megachurch counted 25,000 members in their main location in Atlanta. With three services and satellite services elsewhere, they were easily reaching 75,000 people each week. This gentleman was insistent that I meet the senior pastor.

I was invited to Atlanta, where I would speak at a small church and then be introduced to the senior pastor. I was immediately comfortable in a relationship with him because he came across as sincere and humble. I needed mentors in my life, and this became a very meaningful moment in my life. Inside, I was saying, "Wow! God still has a desire to use me." I had been stepping out in small things, not seeking anything large. I was not sending resumes, interviewing, auditioning, or doing anything grandiose, yet amazing things were starting to happen.

After initially meeting the senior pastor, I returned to Indiana, where I started a Bible study of my own. That Bible study grew and turned into a church. We had our own facility and amazing things were happening.

In 2009, I received a message that the senior pastor wanted me to come to Atlanta. At this point, we had been in communication for four to five years. I was invited to come, but I had no idea why or what was happening at the service I was asked to attend.

I found myself on a plane flying to Atlanta with no idea why, other than the senior pastor had requested my presence. I had one suit with me and an outfit to change into. I presumed I was going for the day and perhaps a meeting. When I arrived, they took me to a hotel and gave me a room. I was told that someone was going to come by later to get me. I was also told to "consecrate myself." I was not sure exactly what that was supposed to mean, but it sounded so spiritual. I was hungry from having been traveling but guessed I should not eat. Maybe "consecrating myself" meant I should be fasting and praying.

There were other pastors there at the hotel, and they, too, had been given the invitation to come without any clear reason why. There was a confused silence among us. Eventually, a woman knocked on the hotel room door. She and a gentleman entered and put a flower on my lapel, and they told me the car was going to take me over to the church in a moment. I was still unsure what was going on and became even more confused as they began to speak of being honored to have me here and be with me. They went on to say, "God is going to do an amazing thing in you." I sort of nodded and offered an insincere, "Thank you." All the while, a single thought was going through my head: "I wish someone would tell me why I am here."

During conversations with the other pastors, I learned that one of them called off his honeymoon to be there among the twelve of us. Obviously, we all felt compelled to drop everything when the senior pastor requested our presence.

We arrived at the church and were taken to a private room. We could hear people beginning to fill the church sanctuary. In the private room, people continued coming up to us and talking to us in the most heartfelt way, repeating the theme that this was such a big moment, and they were honored to be a part of it with us. My confusion continued as I halfheartedly said, "Thank you. Thank you," and tried to get answers by tacking on, "What is it about?" receiving nothing more than "Oh, you will see" in return.

During the five years I had known the senior pastor, I had met several of the other pastors in the group of twelve. Looking around at them, I asked, "Do you know what we are here for?" The resounding answer was "No." At this point, we were simply speculating. We realized it must be some kind of service. Perhaps there would be something special going on that night.

Eventually, they took us downstairs and led us into the sanctuary. The place was packed. People were dressed formally in their Sunday best. The music and the singing in the air were moving. It reminded me of many years earlier in college when I went to a Promise Keepers rally. At the rally, all the men were singing in unison as a group of us were walking into the arena. It felt like an earthquake as the bass voices literally shook the atmosphere. Even the floors shook. Fifty thousand men singing "Amen" can move a building. I couldn't help but pause and imagine what heaven would be like. I had a flashback as that same feeling returned as I was entering the sanctuary at the megachurch.

As the service began, I still didn't know why I was there, and then my name was called, Pastor James Dixon. I went forward and stood with the other pastors whose names were also being called. The senior pastor stood up and began to speak. He then addressed us,

"I know you do not know why you are here, but I am making you 'Ambassadors.'"

There I was standing in front of this church at both highs and lows in my life. My personal low was fighting custody battles and struggling with people who seemed to love position but not me. In contrast, I was experiencing the high of returning to ministry in full force. Externally, I wanted to do things. I was ready. I knew my gifting is my ability to speak. I was starting a church, yet internally I was struggling. Could I preach knowing that I am prone to wander? The more I found myself running from it, the more I found myself serving. Ministry was expanding, but not by my pursuing it. My heart was saying, "Lord, I do not want to let you down." but my humanness lacked confidence. The senior pastor was introducing us to this massive congregation as future leaders of the world. In my mind, I was thinking, "This has to be a mistake, me?"

That night, the senior pastor spoke over my life. "You have come to upset systems. You have come to walk big, bad, and bold into the enemy's camp to set captives free. God has called you to a particular group of people. This is international." His endorsement was huge, even though it was just human. Everything he said was an echo of other things people had been saying throughout my life.

I boarded the plane back to Indiana carrying a plaque saying I had been ordained by him, one of twelve men he ordained that weekend.

THE FALL

During my time with the megachurch pastor, I attended a march in Atlanta where Martin Luther King's daughter lit a torch from the eternal flame at the King Center and handed it to him. "The Eternal Flame symbolizes the continuing effort to realize Dr. King's dream of the 'Beloved Community,' which was his vision for a world of justice, peace, and equality for all mankind." (thekingcenter.org) The senior pastor handed that torch to me, and then I passed it to several other pastors who were with us. He said, "What killed King was that one man tried to carry the dream. If one man does, it is too much, but if we all carry our crosses, we can touch so many more. It cannot be about one man, because if one man falls, we would all fall." At the time, I did not realize how true and how prophetic those words were.

Back in Indiana, things were growing and going well. In 2010, I was asked to be the keynote speaker for the church service for the

Indiana Black Expo, the largest gathering of black people in America. It was the fortieth anniversary of the event. There would be 60,000 black people coming together on that weekend, and I was to lead the church service. What an amazing honor this would be.

I requested my megachurch senior pastor come and speak. He was supposed to be on vacation, but he canceled everything to join me. He had just released a book and would be bringing copies of it. I was feeling like a proud son and was getting to bring this well-known man who had been my mentor and role model in ministry. This was a huge opportunity because the entire demographic I was trying to reach in my home state would be there. What a launch for my own ministry! In a fleshly way, it felt like a "this is my son, in whom I am well pleased" moment. With the endorsement of this pastor, I would likely have hundreds, if not thousands, of people follow me and become members of my church. This was going to be great.

The night before the service, some young people were shot downtown in black-on-black violence. I was asked to speak to the media, and I agreed to do it. As I was being interviewed, the interviewer asked about a breaking story related to the pastor. I felt like I was being set up for the "shock and awe" moment. I questioned whether the interview had anything to do with the violence or if that was just a cover to get me in front of a camera because of my affiliation with the senior pastor and the service with him scheduled for the next day.

I thought I was so smart and thought I had everything covered. Normally, the speaker fee would have been tens of thousands of dollars for the megachurch pastor. Because of our relationship, I was going to get a rate far less than that. I had arranged for businesses to sponsor a luncheon to meet and discuss business opportunities, and those funds would cover the speaking fee. I had worked every angle I could through relationships and had sacrificed so much to pull off something this massive. This was looking like a big win, and suddenly it was all crumbling. The chips were in, and now for the house to call cheating on the biggest win for me was a rough one. We went into defense mode.

He had been my connection for meeting so many famous people and had been among America's best loved African American pastors, and now he was reduced to nothing.

There had been times I could get a phone call to fill in for him if he could not speak somewhere. I might drive as far as South Carolina to speak on his behalf. Without hesitation, I would fill in for a pastor at the church. I had been in the midst of all the amazing things God was doing, and now it was crumbling.

It felt like the demise of the ministry as the congregation, once numbering 25,000, dwindled to hundreds. It was not so much the loss of bodies in the seats that was hardest to watch. There were people who walked away from God. Sometimes, people associate an individual's sin with God because of that individual's position, and it has nothing to do with Him. Humans mess up, which is why ultimate trust must be in God, not a church leader.

So many people in ministry had begged to be in the pastor's inner circle. They had wanted to get to know him. I personally had so many pastors approach me, hoping I could introduce them to him or get them a photo opportunity with him, but then they turned and walked away. So many relationships were left tainted or broken. What I really learned walking through that season was it is not about a man. It is not about fandom, stardom, or celebrity status. It is not about you, but about what God chooses to do with you in your assignment. It is not about the size of your church or the megaphone in your hand. It is about submitting to God, repenting from sin, and staying away from that sin.

Ministry is not about chasing opportunities, but simply walking in the things God puts in front of me. It is not about going to a certain place or being around certain people. It is not about who I know or a Rolodex or name dropping. What God has planned is so much greater than we can think or imagine; so, simply taking the steps of obedience right in front of me will turn into something totally different, something much more powerful.

God showed me the modern-day version of 1 Kings 19:11-12. Elijah was seeking answers from God and was given directions. "'Go out and stand on the mountain in the presence of the Lord, for the Lord is about to pass by.' Then a great and powerful wind tore the mountains apart and shattered the rocks before the Lord, but the Lord was not in the wind. After the wind, there was an earthquake, but the Lord was not in the earthquake. After the earthquake came a fire, but the Lord was not in the fire. And after the fire came a gentle whisper." God was in the whisper.

God was teaching me that it was important for me to establish relationships with great humble men who would serve God and hold each other accountable. For a season, our egos had been in the way, and we all wanted to have a church with the name of the megachurch on it or be an affiliate or associate of it. We learned to use the church name God gave us and focus on Him. Big churches are an instrument. They are not the source. We must serve in humility and keep Him as our source.

"SECULAR" WORK

I had started ministry again, and it was growing; but, at the same time, I was struggling. Everyone else seemed to see potential in me, but I could not see it in myself. I had been ordained in a church with 25,000 members during some of the very lowest moments of my life. People were saying all these great things I would be and do, but I struggled to believe it was even possible. All of it was echoing the same mantra and message that God has plans for me and that there are particular people whom I am supposed to reach. I heard this when I got saved. I heard it when I was in college. I was hearing it again now but was not sure how it would ever come to pass. The struggle was unrelenting. If they can see it, why can't I? I once again left the ministry in anger and frustration at my Savior.

I was struggling in my relationship with God, and thus working full time in ministry was going to be a challenge. I needed an income to cover child support and responsibilities, so I went looking for a "regular" job. The only employer hiring at the time was a membership-only box store, and the only position they had open was pushing carts. On my first day, as I was pushing the carts, I noticed people were staring at me in a way that I felt my self-esteem taking a hit. I was confusing my role and my identity. My role of pushing the carts was somehow in the way of my identity. I thought that somehow it made me less of a man; but I needed this job so I could not quit. I felt I needed to validate myself, and recognizing people I knew who were now seeing me pushing carts felt embarrassing. I believe God was testing me to see how I could handle being humbled.

On the second day, I came to work wearing a suit and pushed the same carts. While I was overdressed for the job of pushing carts, it made people approach me like I was the manager. They would ask me questions, and I would walk into the store to get them the answers. I had not shopped at this store, but gradually learned more about it.

Since the store was a membership-only place, I started giving people tours, and they would sign up. The number of new member signups increased dramatically, and I might personally be responsible for more than two dozen on a weekend. Apparently, I was setting company records. As far as I was concerned, I was just honoring my employer and doing my job with excellence. The success my location was experiencing caught the attention of people at corporate, so they sent a team to find out how the guy on the carts was beating the performance goals of the people specifically hired on a full=time basis to increase memberships.

Certain people were becoming jealous and making comments, but it didn't stop me. I was hired in December, and in January, I was employee of the month. I remember a coworker noting how hard I was working, even though I was only making twelve dollars an hour. She made more than double that. Two months later, I was her boss's boss.

The corporate team decided to mimic my techniques and rolled them out around the country. The new membership revenue became significant for the company and greatly improved profits. The success and recognition for my success were encouraging, but I was trading my gift of evangelism once again for commercial and economic gain. I was using the gifts and talents God gave me for persuading people, but it was not fulfilling. While in a span of just two months, my income had increased three and a half times what it was initially, there was still no purpose or joy in it. Now that I was in management with great pay, I was working so many hours, but it came at a cost. My children would come to spend the weekend with me; however, I was working. My mother would drive them over to the store, and I would spend an hour with them. The job was costing me my relationships with my children. I decided I needed a change. I had to do something different.

Since my family had always worked in factories, I decided I would become part of the third generation working in the automotive industry. All the people who were significant in my life had set an example of working multiple decades for these employers. I would carry on the legacy of my grandfather on my father's side, my grandmother on my mother's side, and my mother. It was challenging to get in the door of this employer, so my best chance was through a referral from someone who already worked there. When I got the job, I promised I would "represent." I would work hard and do well.

I was given the opportunity to start as a temp. The work was hard. There was a lot of walking and moving in ways for which my prosthetic was not designed. I had ancient prosthetics. I had always struggled up to this point to accept that I was an amputee and, thus, had neglected some of the basic care I should have pursued. I did not go to the prosthetist as often as I should have. I had ingrained myself in the able world so much that I had neglected some of my own care.

When I did go to the prosthetist, he did not see my potential, so he didn't suggest any different solutions. I was not actively advocating for myself, primarily because I was not aware of what I did not know. There I was working in a factory doing high-level work with a low-level leg. The leg was never designed for the stress I was putting it under and inevitably it broke. Unfortunately, I was a temp and did not have health insurance. Health insurance or not, I needed this job, so I had to do something. Sometimes, survival necessitates creativity and resourcefulness and, thus, I used electrical tape to keep my prosthetic together.

My makeshift solution was not ideal. I walked more than seventeen miles a day and stood as often as ten hours per shift. At the end of the day, my leg hurt. When I went home, I would soak my leg in Epsom salts in an attempt to get the leg to feel better, or at least well enough that I could do it all over again the next day. For four years, I was without insurance and made do with the electrical tape solution and daily routine with the Epsom salts.

Even with all the pain, I still had an interest in fitness. Every day after work, I would go to the gym and work out. It was just what I did.

I had seen an infomercial about elevation masks, and it showed people working out while wearing them. The mask was designed to simulate training at high altitudes where there is less oxygen. It was supposed to strengthen the respiratory muscles for both improved aerobic and anaerobic performance. The stamina, endurance, strength, and power it boasted I would gain had me sold, so I ordered one.

My job was basically one big workout, so why not add the elevation mask to double up on the physical benefits. I brought it to work and decided to tackle my eight-hour high-paced job while wearing the elevation mask. I put on the mask, put my music in my headphones, and started my day. It was not long before I realized it was really hard to breathe. I was determined and challenged myself to not give up. I knew I was in shape, but I was really struggling.

I woke up in an ambulance. I did not know that the valves on the mask came closed, which effectively means you cannot breathe at all. I didn't know you needed to open them up and had simply put it on and started working. As a result, I nearly suffocated myself. My enthusiasm without direction almost killed me.

Thanks to me, my employer created a rule that you could not wear a mask while working. The pandemic necessitated a slight change to that policy.

Once again, I had people coming into my life, saying, "You are not supposed to be here. I do not know where you are supposed to be, but not here. God has something else for you." In my head, I was saying, "Not this again." God had a way of continually putting U-turns along my path. One thing I have learned is the longer you wait to get there, the harder it is to find your off ramp and get back going the right way. It is easy to become ingrained and entrenched in a lifestyle, a job, and a sense of security. I had moved up in the automotive company and was making great money. I was getting significant bonuses. Why would I ever want to leave that? Surely, I could still do this and whatever God wanted. Surely, I could negotiate with God, and He could have my off time.

I was starting to make videos of my workouts as an amputee. Of course, I had to dress the part and walked into a sporting goods store. It "just so happened" that a gentleman from a fitness clothing company was at the store. He saw me walk in the door and asked me to do that again. At the time, the Rock was releasing a new line of clothes, and my dimensions were the same as his, 6'4" 260 lbs. The gentleman had noticed my silhouette and how similar I looked to the Rock. This "chance encounter" led to me becoming a fitness clothing model.

Things were changing at work, and certain clauses around the issue of preexisting conditions were being rewritten. My employer held a health fair, and two prosthetic provider clinics came in to show what they could offer to someone like me. I connected with one of them and was able to get a new leg, which marked the beginning of a whole new life.

For the first time, my leg wasn't hurting. There was finally a solution, and I felt I could do things. I was excited. I had been working out regularly, and now I felt invincible.

36

THE RACE

I learned there was a race scheduled just two days after I received my leg and decided I would do it. It was to be a 5K, and with my walking as much as seventeen miles a day at work, just over three miles sounded easy. I bought a brand-new pair of shoes the day before the race and was confident I could finish and probably even win. I was near the front of the line to register when I realized I had been in error about the distance of the race. This was not, in fact, a 5K, but rather a full marathon.

Upon hearing the words full marathon, I was going to back out, but now I had a new problem. I had been doing the workout videos and had appeared in some advertisements, so now people were recognizing me. There were other amputees there, ready to cheer me on. With all these people there and some ego on the line, there was no way I could back out. My mom was there with my two sons. I had always told them not to quit, so I could not quit without even trying.

I started thinking about how to get out of this situation. Perhaps I could start the race and when I got out of sight of these people, I could quit. Inevitably, throughout the race, when I thought there was a chance to escape unseen, someone would be right there who knew me, or there would be another amputee cheering me on. As I ran, one thing became very apparent to me, my prosthetic side was not hurting. For the first time in my life, I started feeling fatigue in my sound leg. How could it be that now my left leg was giving me problems? It had never known fatigue. My prosthetic leg had always been my "Achilles heel."

All those questions about "What if I did not have a bad leg?" were being answered as I was running, so I had to keep going. When I finished, it was not an impressive time by the standards of a regular marathoner, but it was impressive because it was the first time for me. It was also impressive because I never felt pain in my prosthetic side. It was my sound leg that was hurting, and I did not quit.

Since I was feeling like I could do anything, I started doing powerlifting.

For more than 40 years, I had always been held back by my bad leg, and now I wanted to do everything I could think of. I did Cross Fit Games for the first time and finished no worse than third at anything. When it came to powerlifting, I always walked away with a first-place trophy. I didn't even realize I was setting records. I was just doing everything, trying to find out what I could and could not do. I was making up for so much lost time and finding out what I had missed during all those years.

WORKPLACE MINISTRY

As exciting as life was becoming with the new prosthetic, it was still a far cry from doing what God had called me to do, or so I thought.

Since those days of physical education class, I had always avoided wearing shorts because I was embarrassed about my leg. With the new leg and the competitive physical success I was having, I finally had enough internal confidence to wear shorts through the automotive plant. I was embracing being an amputee for the first time at the age of 44. While that was a monumental moment for me, it was also becoming monumental for others. Coworkers were seeing me in shorts and realizing I was an amputee. They started asking me to help other coworkers or their friends or family members affected by amputation. These informal mentoring sessions continued to increase.

Eleven years went by working at the automotive plant, and

someone came into my life and told me, "This is not for you. This is not where you are supposed to be. I don't know where you are supposed to be, but this is not it." This was the ever-repeating anthem throughout my life. "This is not where I am supposed to be."

As far as I was concerned, I had a job. I had elevated into leadership positions. Life was kind of on an easy street for me there. There was no way in the world I should be dissatisfied. I was making a great income. I had the best insurance. I now had a desk job, which doubled as my own workout space.

I had enough flexibility that at times I could take days off work and drive a distance to meet with an amputee. I would then contact the company that made my prosthetic to see if there was a representative nearby who could help this amputee. I started to realize that the joy I was experiencing as I worked with these other amputees was God revealing to me, "James, this is what you are here for." I realized that sometimes a salary is what you are paid to give up your dreams, which is a modified version of Kevin O'Leary's quote, "A salary is the drug they give you to forget your dreams."

THE PROSTHETIC COMPANY

I was becoming well known by the company that designed my new prosthetic leg. The initial leg I had was only rated up to 325 pounds, but with my ability to powerlift, I needed something stronger. The company decided to experiment to see if they could build a custom leg that could stand up to the abilities of my sound leg and the rest of my body. A representative from the prosthetic company came in person to deliver the leg to me. He stayed to watch me test it out. I successfully did the squat with 760 pounds. I felt like we could have done more, but we needed heavier plates. The gym where we did the test only had 45-pound plates, and we had maxed out what the length of the bar could hold. We really needed some 100-pound plates.

Not only had I done one squat with 760 pounds, but I had done five straight reps. I was so excited that not only had I done it, but I learned it was a bar that the prosthetic company did not think could be crossed.

The representative from the prosthetic company who had witnessed the test of the new leg and the record-breaking success knew I was a fitness clothing model and asked if I could get my hands on a specific pair of shoes for him. With my friends and family discounts and the effort he had made to help get me this custom leg, it was the least I could do in return.

I had the shoes in hand and arranged to meet him at his hotel on my way to work. He was there to lead a training session with a group of their representatives. When I arrived, he asked if I would come in and say a few words to the guys. As far as I was concerned, I was just dropping off the shoes and heading to work but agreed to stop in at their meeting. I gave an impromptu speech from the heart about the difference they can make in a life and how my high-level prosthetic changed my life. I educated them on what I could have done had I known about the technology sooner. I challenged them to do even more for others than they did for me. When I left the room, there was not a dry eye.

Apparently, after I left, those in the room said they wished they could hear more from me. As I was driving to work, my phone rang. My prosthetic company point of contact asked me if I would be willing to come to different cities to speak to the various teams. I gave a casual, "Sure." As I was pulling into the parking lot at work, the phone rang again, and I was told that plan was canceled. It was another casual, "That's okay." I had gotten my hopes up and realized I had genuinely enjoyed those moments speaking to and inspiring the prosthetics' sales team. He clarified the reason for the cancellation, "We want you to speak at our national event." That was completely unexpected. In a matter of minutes after a short speech from the heart, I went from the idea of going to speak to small groups to speaking at the national event.

When I went to the national event, I was told by my contact's boss that I was the best speaker he had ever heard and that I should do this full time. It was a bit surreal, and all I could say was, "Yeah. I appreciate that." His words proved to be almost prophetic because, sure enough, I started traveling and speaking. Additionally, opportunities for newspaper and magazine articles started coming.

As time passed, I encountered children I had met years earlier when they could not walk, who were now successfully walking because I had connected them with a great prosthetist who actively pursued the right solution for them. Seeing them walking and thriving put a smile on my face. My heart was overflowing with joy as I served fellow amputees and saw them achieve breakthroughs not unlike my own.

In April of 2022, I was able to leave my automotive industry job to pursue my life's purpose full-time. I might have broken the lineage of generations who gave their whole futures to that industry, but God used that season of my life to be another steppingstone into His purpose for me. God had been directing me not just to speak for Him, but to speak to a particular group of people, other amputees. I have been called to embrace the thing that I thought He cursed me with. I now realize it was my blessing.

The habits that I started as a child, working out with the Hulk Hogan weight set, was the foreshadowing of one of the things that would actually open doors for me. The lifting of heavy physical weights is almost symbolic of my real purpose of lifting people. I had always wanted to motivate people to become more and to serve God. I have realized that He needed me to become more first.

The more I have stepped out in obedience to Him, the more doors have opened, and opportunities have come.

My social media presence took off because of a simple 19-second clip of me talking about God and how He works. I was heading to the gym and just wanted to record something quickly. I was speaking from Luke 8:17, which says, "For there is nothing hidden that will not be disclosed, and nothing concealed that will not be known or brought out into the open." Oftentimes, that verse is used in the context of the sin in our lives being exposed, but it can also be true about the positive things we do in life. It goes both ways. The things we do for Him in private will show up in public. What we do in the dark will come to the light.

While it was being aired across social media, I was really speaking to myself. The things I have done in the dark that were wrong had already done their damage. I am thankful God can bring forth crop failure on the damaging seeds you sow in your life and am thankful for how the right things I had been doing that no one saw are finally bearing good fruit. All the working out, speaking into the lives of others, building my confidence, embracing my disability, and realizing that my disability is a gift that God has given me is finally bringing forth fruit that can be seen.

Everything that is happening is happening organically. I have not been sending out my resume or searching things out. There really is not a job description for what I do. The prosthetic company asked me, "What do we call what you do? It is not a job with set qualifications or a required degree." From my vantage point, God said, "I have trained you so that the qualifications you have are not on paper. The qualifications were gained through the trials and tribulations of your life."

Sometimes I think, "What if I had embraced being an amputee sooner?" But then I realize I would not have the sense of urgency that I have today. I truly enjoy being a patient emissary or ambassador. I think back to when I was given the title of "Ambassador" when ordained and how God has a sense of humor.

I never have a normal day. My phone might ring, and the caller says, "We have a gentleman who is going to lose his leg this afternoon. Can you talk to him?" To one of these calls, I asked, "Where are you?" The answer, "Michigan." The next question, "How did you hear about me?" The answer is nothing short of God's divine hand at work. "My mom heard about you through a friend of hers who works out and saw a video of yours." These calls lead to so many opportunities to pray with people and share Jesus in moments of desperate need.

I have been called into life-and-death situations. I was called to minister to a woman who wanted to harm herself. To later hear her say, "James, you restored hope in me," was priceless. When I met her, all she could say was, "James, I'm broken." I gave her a hug and told her, "God is not done with you yet. Everything that you have gone through, He can use for good. What the devil meant for evil, God can use for good. It can be a blessing to you, but you have to get to a point where you can be free, open, and honest about it. Tell God that it hurts."

Sometimes, when you are in the middle of a situation, you cannot see how anything good can come of it. Healing and time may bring you to a place where you can see and be thankful for the good that came, even through bad things and bad circumstances.

I encouraged her, "You can thank God for getting you out of a bad situation. Yes, you may have been taken advantage of as a child, but He preserved your life so you can get beyond it. You can say, 'I did not think I would get out of their control but, God, you got me out of there so they can no longer harm me.' If you ever see the people who harmed you again, you will show them they have no power over you as they see you surviving and thriving. They get to see that you are bigger than those past moments. They get to see what victory looks like. You get to go back big, bad, and tough, knowing that God is able to beat whatever plan the devil had using them in the past. You don't have to forgive them on your own. You just have to go to God and say, 'Please help me to release the hatred for the things that happened. I give that to You, and I give them to You. I will not seek vengeance because if I beat them up, I will go to jail.'"

God's vengeance is worse than anything you could dream up. If you think their lives have not been tormented since that day, or if they have had a peaceful night's sleep, or if their consciences have not sat on a pulpit and talked to them, then you are missing it. This life is so quick, and they will step off into eternity. If they have not found Jesus, those moments will be relived forever. Luke 17:2 says, "It would be better for them to be thrown into the sea with a millstone tied around their neck than to cause one of these little ones to stumble."

Sometimes, my role is just to encourage people in their journey. I was at an event and met a young, 25-year-old mom who was new to the world of parenting a child with a limb difference. She was vulnerably honest as she said, "I do not know what I am doing. Help me, please." She was already doing one of the best things she could do. She was putting herself and her child in the path of amputees who are living full and rewarding lives, which gives her a vision for what can be for her child. She was taking the initiative to seek out and learn from those who have already walked on the road she is beginning.

My job is to be God's vessel to restore hope. That hope is physical in the practical connecting and coaching as it relates to a prosthetic. That hope is also emotional and spiritual as I share the love of Jesus and the joy of salvation. While I could be tempted to let ego get in the way, the truly great thing about people looking to me is it affirms that God is still using me. It has been such a blessing to minister to fellow amputees and their families.

ADVICE FOR THE NEW AMPUTEE

If you are a new amputee or a friend or family member of a new amputee, here are some thoughts to hopefully allow you to skip over some of the lessons I learned through the "school of hard knocks." Obviously, my life experience is as a single leg, below the knee amputee, so some of this may or may not apply directly to your specific situation.

The first thing to do is to seek out an advocate. There are people who have been through what you are about to face. There are organizations that can help you advocate for yourself and can connect you to others who have traveled a road similar to yours. It is your body and your life, so there is no one else who has as much to gain or lose as you. No one will fight that battle for you like you will. You will need to learn, and you will need to research. It is wise to find someone who is fully active, fully acclimated, and proud of who they are. They can be a great source of advice on how to deal with and overcome situations.

Having an amputation is like having a personal funeral that other people do not want to attend. You are losing a part of yourself, and, as a result, you can end up with self-doubt and body dysmorphia. It is important to have someone to encourage you and to be there with you throughout the process. Advocacy is family.

I experienced my amputation as a child, and children grow constantly and fast, which often means they may not get the highest quality prosthetic. For me, something was considered better than nothing. My prosthetic had a rubber foot, which was very heavy, and the leg did not have any give or flexibility in it. This presented challenges for a child who desired to be active. Anytime someone hit the front of my foot, which could happen doing normal things with other kids, it would dislocate my kneecap, and I would have to go to the hospital. I developed fears about how active I could be.

Today, the technology exists for high activity limbs. Today's children should not receive a leg like what you would find on a mannequin in a department store. I encourage parents to actively advocate for the best possible solution for their child. Insurance may be a challenge, but there are also grants and legitimate medical fundraising organizations worth researching.

Support groups are critical, not just for the amputee but also for family members who need to stay engaged without enabling the person. The amputee will have to learn to do things in new ways to regain their independence. If a leg has been lost, they will have to relearn to walk. They will have to learn to go from wheelchair to walker to cane to walking without assistance. There may be a point when forward progression stops, and part of advocacy is to be there to support, regardless of the outcomes.

There are some key things to keep in mind when talking to a prosthetist. The prosthetist may ask, "What activities would you like to do?" What they are actually doing is using the insurance company guides to classify you. You could be a K-0,1, 2, 3, or 4. Every full-bodied person is a K3. A K4 is an elite athlete who can do almost anything. A small child is generally a K4. I am a K4.

When they ask you what activities you want to do, you might say, "I want to walk my dog." You should not simply say, "I want to walk my dog." You need to be more descriptive and specific so that they fit you with the correct prosthetic for the activities of your life. You should talk about the size of the dog. For example, "I walk a 22-pound Shih Tzu on a leash, and it is important that I not trip and fall. I need to have good balance, and I need to have an energy-return leg so I can walk distances with my dog." The more activities you have and the more descriptive you are, the better the prosthetic. Instead of just saying you go on a walk, you might say, "I walk on uneven terrain. Sometimes, there might be pebbles in my pathway or hills to go up and down. There might be different surfaces that I experience." This information contributes to the level of prosthetic for which you qualify.

As you progress, do not let them stick you with a walker and say that is a walking apparatus. Make sure your leg is being cared for and you get the best quality prosthetic. You might describe that your activities include the need to carry things in and out of your house. A walker would not allow you the active use of your hands to carry things, so they must give you a prosthetic.

Not all amputees will get a prosthetic, so it is critical that you advocate for yourself. It is an unfortunate reality that not everyone can afford to get what they need, but do not give up the fight. If you do nothing, you are guaranteed to get nothing. Become an advocate and fight to get what you need!

There are vacuum, suction, and pin prosthetics. Learning the differences is important. There are advantages for different situations and reasons why you should seek them out. The sockets matter, and the types of tools that are attached matter. You want to preserve your good leg or, as we call it, sound leg. Your prosthetic can be designed with energy return, and the energy return can also save your spine and hips from damage. Doing your research, working with a good advocate, and seeking out lots of counsel will help you get the best solution for you.

If you are diabetic or you have issues with wounds, you need to research the different type of prosthetics that are suggested for amputees in your situation. A vacuum system prosthetic would be worth researching because it serves like a hyperbaric chamber, and it will promote healing as you are walking and living. Revisions are not the preferred way to address a sore. If an amputee gets a sore, it is not uncommon that they won't do anything other than suggest that they take their prosthetic off. The danger is that you will atrophy, decondition, and get depressed because you cannot walk.

Prosthetists have different skill levels. They may direct you down the path of what is easiest for them or most profitable for them. That may or may not be what is best for you, so being your own advocate and researching is important. Also, when selecting a prosthetist, it is important to find a place that has a full team that is continuously learning. Going to a one-stop shop with one guy can be risky. He may be a wonderful one guy, but he is just one guy. If you ask your one-guy prosthetist, "What is your plan in five years?" and he says, "Hopefully, I am retired and living in Florida," he may not be the right person for you. He is likely not going to be there when you need him. You need to pick a place where you can get long-term care for the balance of your life, not just for one prosthetic. You need to ask yourself this question, "Can they know me, know my story, grow with me as I grow, and change with me as I change?"

Beware if the prosthetist says, "Let's start off with this leg, and in a few years, we will go back and get a different leg or make changes if needed." There is no guarantee that insurance is going to give you a better leg later. It would be better to get the higher end leg and water down from it later, than to start low and hope that one day you will get a higher quality leg. It would take a lot of proven activities and documentation from your rehab to go up in quality.

There are many options around wearing shoes with prosthetics; however, it is critical to evaluate the pitches of the shoes because it changes your gait as you walk. Having an experienced mentor to help you is important. It is not necessarily about having the most comfortable shoes because the prosthetic can't feel the shoe, but what you can feel is if the arch is too elevated, and it forces you to compensate unnaturally.

Phantom pains are real. Nerves have been severed and, at times, they may become confused and communicate to the brain that there is an active issue that needs to be addressed. There are techniques to address phantom pains. There is medication, but there are also non-medicating means to deal with them. One technique is mirror therapy. You look in the mirror at the leg you still have—by looking at the reflection, your mind sees both legs still there. While looking in the mirror, you massage the sound leg, and your mind is tricked into thinking it is the missing leg. This technique may alleviate some of the pain.

It is wise to ask your physical therapist or prosthetist when a good time is, after your amputation, to start massaging your residual limb. Your residual limb has scar tissue, and massaging helps break that up.

When you go to the prosthetist, you might not want to completely disrobe; so, finding adaptive clothing where you can unzip the pant leg or roll it up easily is a good option. Tear-away sweats are another possibility.

If you were very athletic before or are looking for a new goal given your new situation, research and get involved with adaptive athletics. I never knew about the Paralympics because other than seeing other amputees in the hospital, I never saw any in my daily life. Because I had always competed against able-bodied students and was very strong, I likely could have competed in a Paralympics had I known about it. Getting involved in adaptive athletics is a great way to maintain physical abilities and develop meaningful social connections. I never saw amputees represented in athletics, advertising, or television; but, fortunately, today mainstream media has become more aware of us.

It is important to get involved in the amputee community for the practical elements of advice and ideas, but also for the mental and emotional benefits of comradery and support. Organizations like the Challenged Athletes Foundation and trade shows like the Abilities Expos are great places to start. Being exposed to and seeing other people who are like you and living their best life is important. As a child, I did not have that, and I value it today.

SUPERMAN

I was at a Challenged Athletes Foundation event and met a five-year-old boy who had never seen another amputee. He was now in an environment surrounded by people just like him. All the other kids were loving on him, even ones with more challenging situations than him. I was assigned to assist him in the race, and as his mom pushed him in his wheelchair across the finish line to get his medal, she yelled out, "We will never forget you, Superman." On a human level, there is nothing that can beat that warm feeling in my heart, but even more than meeting Superman, me, I want people to meet the real Superman in my life.

Superman began as a nickname in childhood as my mom and grandma worked to instill in me the confidence that I could rise above my disability and become something great. As I grew older and my physical strength became apparent, Superman took on a more literal meaning. Today, Superman is not about me. Superman is about Jesus. My attachment to Jesus has been my breakthrough in life. My tag line, Superman is 4 Real, has nothing to do with the film but has everything to do with my becoming real with my faith and realizing that the loss of my limb was the gain of my purpose. Superman is 4 Real because Jesus is for real. My 40-plus years of delay was not that God was rejecting or abandoning me, but that I needed to go through training to be what He has called me to be. You cannot take on a big task if you cannot handle the small tasks. I had to learn to handle the small tasks. You must be willing to endure. You must put in the work. You must sense the urgency and realize that you do not have time to waste.

If I were to encounter you in person, I would want to introduce you to Superman. I might ask you, "Are you a Christian?" If you responded that you are, then I would ask the follow-up question, "How did you become one?" If you responded that you come from a family of church people or grew up in the church, I would ask the clarifying question, "If I stood in the garage and perfected how to say "Beep. Beep," would that make me a car?"

I have often heard people confuse church attendance with what it means to truly be a Christian. Just as I saw acted out in the Heaven's Gates and Hell's Flames play, I would ask you how you would answer God if He asked you, "Why should I let you into Heaven?" The reasons you previously gave about coming from a family of church people or growing up in church are not valid. What other answer can you give? If you say because you have done good works, which I do respect, I present this scenario to you. We have a long jump contest across the Grand Canyon. Jesus is the first to go, and He successfully jumps the whole way across. That is an impossible jump for all of us to make. What if all your good works could be stacked up to help you get across? How do you feel compared to Mother Theresa, better or worse? You would likely say, "She was better than me." She runs, jumps, makes it halfway and falls because of one sin. How would Hitler do? He would not do well at all based on good works. He immediately falls off the cliff. Even if I am better than Hitler, but worse than Mother Theresa, I am still a far cry from Jesus. To cross that gap, I must accept Jesus.

Only Jesus can take you from where you are and get you to God. You must accept the work that He has already done. My work is not enough. It is too flawed. Your work is not enough. It is too flawed. One sin, if I only did one, is enough to qualify me as a sinner. He is sinless. To get to where He is, I need His help. The only way I get His help is if He creates a pathway and gives me a lifeline. The lifeline He gave was that He laid his life down in exchange for mine. My guilty plea of sin is exchanged for His innocence. He did my time. He offers forgiveness, and He offers His pleas before God for anyone who accepts Him.

I would ask you, "Is there another way outside of accepting Jesus that you can get to God?" If there is not, I beg of you to think about this, if you were to die today, where would you go? There is no reason for us to go to hell. The Bible says that God created hell for the devil and his angels. It was never intended for you and me to go there. Heaven was made for us to fellowship with God. Jesus came to reconnect me and you to Him. God has offered a solution of forgiveness for every wrong and for everything that has happened to us on earth. He is the forgiver, the balm, and the healer.

Jesus takes away all our failings, but to access all those benefits, you have to first accept Him as your Savior. The Bible says in Romans 10:9 that if I confess with my mouth and believe in my heart that God has raised Jesus from the dead, then I will be saved. If I ask

Him to be my personal Lord and Savior and forgive me of my sins, and I mean that with sincerity, then I do not need to jump across that gap. I just need to accept His reached out hand, and He pulls me to the other side. Jesus will stand with me before God and say I made the jump because of Him. Every accusation that has ever been brought against me, even the true ones, has been washed away. Have I lied before? Yes. Have I done things of which I am ashamed? Yes. But there is no condemnation in Christ if I accept him. He forgives me. Even though I am forgiven, I might still have the earthly consequences and ramifications for my sin. If I was smoking or doing drugs for years and ruined my lungs or other organs as a result, even if I accept Jesus and quit, I may still have to live with the physical consequences. I may also still have legal consequences of sin to deal with in this life. I do not suddenly become perfect, but I am forgiven. I am saved, and I have access to God through Christ.

There are no specific magical words to pray to accept Jesus because it is you making a decision in your heart and communicating that decision to Him. If you feel like you need words to guide your communication, here is a sample prayer.

Dear Lord, I am coming to You, realizing that I feel lost, distant, and separated from You because of my sin. I am asking that You come into my life, fill my voids, be my Lord, be my Savior, and forgive my sins. I am asking that Jesus Christ take dominion over my life and help me become more like Him every day going forward. Thank You for hearing my prayer and accepting me as Your child.

In Jesus Name, I pray, Amen.

If you prayed that prayer with sincerity, you probably feel like a burden has been lifted and joy has entered your heart. The joy is not just with you, but Luke 15:7 says Heaven is rejoicing with you. It is important for you, just as it was for me after I accepted Jesus at the Heaven's Gate and Hell's Flames' night, to find a Bible-believing church where you can learn, grow, and become fruitful.

Jesus is quoted in John 15:1-8, "I am the true vine, and my Father is the gardener. He cuts off every branch in me that bears no fruit, while every branch that does bear fruit, He prunes so that it will be even more fruitful. You are already clean because of the word I have spoken to you. Remain in me, as I also remain in you. No branch can bear fruit by itself; it must remain in the vine. Neither can you bear fruit unless you remain in me. I am the vine; you are the branches. If you remain in me and I in you, you will bear much fruit; apart from me, you can do nothing. If you do not remain in me, you are like a branch that is thrown away and withers; such branches are picked up, thrown into the fire and burned. If you remain in me and my words remain in you, ask whatever you wish, and it will be done for you. This is to my Father's glory, that you bear much fruit, showing yourselves to be my disciples."

God is the gardener, Jesus is the vine, and I am one of His branches. I am a branch that spent more time than I should have in the dirt of life and was pruned, literally in my leg while at Shriners, so that I could become more fruitful. I know I am redeemed and called for a purpose. I am both honored and humbled as I see it unfolding before me. I am blessed to have the opportunity to travel the country, speaking to large groups and to individuals one on one. I do not need lights and cameras because it is all about Jesus. I am living proof that He still uses people who feel like they have been abandoned and forgotten and have messed up too many times. His grace and mercy are sufficient.

My fruit is the impact I am having on the lives of others. I particularly love the impact for my fellow amputees who, like me, are finding their way to active, exciting, and rewarding lives. For the amputees I mentor, my fruit will live on through them, as they impact the next generation of amputees.

My fruit is also the inspiration, encouragement, and Biblical principles I am able to share through the Absolute Motivation videos. No matter what you have lost or what you have done, you can come out of a dark place and find hope. Jeremiah 29:11 is still true today. "For I know the plans I have for you," declares the Lord, "plans to prosper you and not to harm you, plans to give you hope and a future." The Absolute Motivation videos have given me a larger platform than any church I could have pastored, and I am not limited to a Sunday morning or Wednesday night. My voice can be heard at any time, any day of the week.

When I am recording my pieces, I am alone with my phone, speaking to myself. I am speaking with a voice that knows pain, but today contains love and promise. There was pain in the things I went through, but I have learned to love myself just the way God made me. I am here to encourage, inspire, and challenge listeners to love themselves, love Jesus, and then positively impact the lives of others. We are all just pilgrims passing through; so, if you are peculiar or unique, own it and accept it. God can use it.

Superman James prays that as you have read my story, you have seen the real Superman Jesus shining through. If you were not on Superman Jesus' team when you started reading, hopefully, you are now. The hurting people in your sphere of influence need a superhero, and you can be the one to introduce them to Superman because Superman is 4 Real.

Luke 15:4-7 says, "Suppose one of you has a hundred sheep and loses one of them. Doesn't he leave the ninety-nine in the open country and go after the lost sheep until he finds it? And when he finds it, he joyfully puts it on his shoulders and goes home. Then he calls his friends and neighbors together and says, 'Rejoice with me; I have found my lost sheep.' I tell you that in the same way there will be more rejoicing in heaven over one sinner who repents than over ninety-nine righteous persons who do not need to repent."

This book might have landed in your hands because you were the "lost sheep." Superman Jesus is the shepherd who has been searching for you. My prayer is that heaven is rejoicing because you have been FOUND.

ABOUT JAMES DIXON

James Dixon is spreading inspiration and empowering souls, one video at a time on the Absolute Motivation YouTube channel.

As an amputee and relentless advocate for all, James ignites the fire within to propel people toward their goals. He is the Keynote Speaker of Absolute Motivation YouTube channel, which dives deep into the realms of personal growth, resilience, and unwavering determination. With a phenomenal community of 1.4 million subscribers, Absolute Motivation is united in their pursuit of excellence. Together, they create a powerful force that uplifts and transforms lives.

Through his journey of overcoming obstacles and embracing challenges head-on, James discovered the limitless potential that resides within each and every one of us. He firmly believes that no matter what circumstances we face, we have the power to rise above, rewrite our stories, and manifest our dreams into reality.

Visit his website: AbsoluteMotivation.tv

Instagram: Supermanis4real

Facebook: James Eltroy Dixon